M000202635

The Need
to be
Liked

by

Dr. Roger Covin

The Need to be Liked
Copyright © Dr. Roger Covin, 2011

All rights reserved. No part of this work may be reproduced, translated, or shared in any form, without the explicit written permission of the copyright owner.

All requests regarding this work are to be made to the copyright owner, who can be reached at the following email address:

roger@drcovin.ca

About the Author

Dr. Roger Covin is a registered psychologist with l'Ordre des Psychologues du Québec. He operates a private practice in the city of Montreal. Dr. Covin earned a B.A. in Psychology from the University College of Cape Breton, and his M.A. and Ph.D degrees in Clinical Psychology from the University of Western Ontario. He completed his residency training with the Calgary Health Region, in Calgary, Alberta. Dr. Covin has published a number of peer-reviewed journal articles and book chapters on various topics in the field of clinical psychology. **The Need to be Liked** is his first book.

Acknowledgments

I would like to thank Allison Ouimet for her invaluable work on this project. And to Norah, for being a bear.

Table of Contents

Chapter 1

INTRODUCTION

As a clinical psychologist, I often work with diverse groups of people. This diversity includes age, race, gender, sexuality, religion, sub cultural affiliations, etc. Each of my clients brings their own unique set of problems to treatment (e.g., depression; anxiety; substance abuse). Given the variety of people I see, both in terms of demographic variables and psychological problems, my sessions can often look quite different from one hour to the next. In one afternoon, I might see a business executive with severe anxiety, followed by a depressed adolescent, followed by a mother of three suffering from Post-Traumatic Stress Disorder (PTSD). However, despite this diversity, I am sometimes struck by the similarity of content discussed in our sessions. Indeed, there is one psychological factor that frequently makes itself evident in our sessions – one that impacts the functioning of each client, regardless of their respective problems -- **the need to be liked** by other people.

This need does not *always* play a role in treatment. There are many psychological factors that must be examined in the course of treatment, but this issue has been discussed with enough regularity that it compelled me to write this book. The need to be liked goes beyond clinical psychology work. I observe the influence of this factor on a daily basis, whether it be through my own interpersonal interactions with people, or through information passed on by popular media. It has also been the subject of numerous research projects, the results of which have helped with my own conceptualizations of what the need to be liked is and how it affects our lives.

The need to be liked plays a tremendous role in shaping people's personalities, impacting upon important decisions related to relationships, work, and hobbies, causing emotional and behavioural problems, and ultimately influencing our quality of life. You may have known someone who was constantly seeking attention, or someone who tended to be overly dependent on others. Examples such as these surround us daily. However, this fundamental human need often operates in more subtle ways than you might think. Indeed, one of the primary goals of this book is to highlight how the need to be liked influences the many facets of our lives in ways that are not always obvious.

My hope is that this book serves an educational function, whereby the reader gets to learn about themselves and others. There is also the potential for this book to serve a therapeutic purpose, or at the very least, open the door to people getting help. As I stated earlier, the need to be liked is often intimately tied to many psychological problems. The last chapter of this book presents strategies for how to reduce and eliminate psychological problems associated with the need to be liked. Thus, another function of this book is to help one section of the readership both identify and change things that are contributing to their current life problems.

However, this is not a "How-To-Be-Liked" book. Overall, the primary focus of the material is on problems and complications that arise from the need to be liked. My goal is for readers to understand what this need is, how it impacts their lives, and to provide some general suggestions for managing problems associated with it.

What is the Need to be Liked?

The need to be liked is a fundamental human need. Everyone has fundamental needs, which impact their lives in significant ways. We know that something is a *fundamental need* if (a) the brain and body are designed to acquire it, and (b) not fulfilling the need has negative effects on the person. Think of food and physical safety. We are designed to need food, and if we don't eat, there are negative consequences (ex: starvation). Similarly, we are designed to keep our bodies safe from harm – the consequences of failing to do so are obvious. From an evolutionary standpoint, the body and brain must operate in such a fashion as to increase the probability of survival. As such, we need the body and brain to know when there are threats to survival. Hence, we feel hunger pangs when we need food, thirst when there's a need for water, and there are a host of mental and physiological reactions associated with keeping us safe from harm. In fact, these reactions to the threat of physical harm will be reviewed in greater detail in Chapter 2 because they are so closely connected with the need to be liked. One of the first goals of this book is to highlight how the need to be liked is a fundamental human need that serves an evolutionary purpose. Chapter 2 reviews what this evolutionary purpose is, and how the human body and brain are designed to serve this purpose.

For now, it is important to start with a general definition of the need to be liked. Essentially, it refers to human beings' motivation to receive a positive evaluation from other people. It is a fundamental human drive that most people are born with, and it is completely normal. Indeed, there is nothing fundamentally wrong with wanting to be liked by other people. For instance, being a likeable person significantly increases the probability of having relationships, which positively impacts our quality of life.

However, problems arise with how this human need is satisfied. The primary focus of this book is on the various ways the need to be liked goes awry – and how it can affect our lives in very negative ways. There are many factors that make the need to be liked a greater struggle than it has to be. Rejection experiences, sensitivity to rejection, dysfunctional beliefs (ex: needing to be liked by everyone), and dysfunctional coping (ex: overcompensating for defects) all serve to complicate the need to be liked. For some people, the whole process of trying to be liked can absolutely ruin their lives. Chapters 3 – 5 review in detail the many problems that arise with needing to be liked. My hope is that the content contained in these chapters provides a psycho-educational function for readers. In other words, I hope readers are able to recognize the ways in which such problems affect their lives.

There is one other concept that should now be introduced, as it will also serve as a focal point of this book. In addition to needing to be liked by other people, it is also important to know *how likeable* you are to other people. Although these two concepts overlap to a great degree, they are distinct. Believing that you are likeable as a person, generally speaking, is very important to mental health and will be discussed throughout the book. In fact, some psychologists are defining self-esteem as the degree to which you believe that you are likeable to others[1].

Beliefs about "likeability," however, do not always correlate with the degree to which someone is actually liked. There are some people who believe they are likeable, yet are not well liked by others. The more common finding is for people to underestimate how likeable they are to other people. Chapter 3 will explain why people do this and what function it serves. Furthermore, Chapter 5 offers a very detailed overview of how the belief of "unlikeability" can significantly shape our behaviour, thoughts, personalities, and relationships with others.

The final chapter of this book can be considered a sort of self-help section. However, this is not a self-help book in the traditional sense of the term. Many legitimate self-help books typically have multiple chapters devoted to specific strategies that can be used to change a particular problem. For example, a self-help book on social anxiety will often have worksheets and various exercises to be used by the reader, and the majority of the book is dedicated to strategies for change. The current book is primarily about describing and articulating how a particular issue affects people's lives in a negative way. This is accomplished by synthesizing contemporary research and theory on this topic with my own clinical experience in order to provide readers with a new way to conceptualize and think about psychological factors. Thus, this book is not simply written for those looking for help — it is also written for people who are simply curious and interested about the need to be liked, including other health professionals. However, for those readers who might like to know more about how to handle the various problems described in this book, Chapter 6 was written to provide this section of the readership with ideas and some strategies as such. For those people who have very serious problems related to interpersonal matters, I strongly recommend they seek the services of a mental health professional.

Chapter 2

THE SOCIAL PROTECTION SYSTEM

For some people, the need to be liked is considered to be an exercise in ego inflation. Getting people to like and love you makes you feel good, and in extreme cases, it allows those with narcissistic characteristics to satisfy a different need – the need to be *admired* by others. However, the need to be liked is deeper in its purpose and function than simply pacifying the cravings of our ego. The need to be liked serves a much greater goal than that – one that is rooted in evolutionary function. The primary function of the need to be liked is to ensure that we form relationships with other people. These relationships can be very close and important (ex: being in love with your spouse) or peripheral and less important (ex: having acquaintances and belonging to groups).

There are people who do not need to be liked, and therefore do not care about relationships, but these people are few and far between. For example, individuals with Schizoid Personality Disorder prefer to not develop relationships with others, and often live in relative isolation. But most of the people on this planet feel compelled to have other people like them, in order to form some sort of attachment. An important question is *why* do we have this need?

To help answer this question, I'm going to briefly discuss another basic human need – the need for physical safety. I am then going to introduce a major psychological factor that is key to this book – social pain. Social pain and the need to be liked are intimately linked. But first, let's examine the need for physical safety, and in particular, the similarities between this need and the need to be liked.

The Need for Physical Safety – Introducing the Physical Protection System

Over the course of time, and by the process of human evolution, people inherited the basic need to seek safety from harm. The reason for needing this inheritance is clear – survival of one's genes improves dramatically when one is physically safe. Therefore, the brain and body are designed to keep people safe. You could say we have a built-in "protection system" that was designed to ensure safety from danger. This *Physical Protection System* consists of multiple parts:

Threat Appraisal

This part of the system is responsible for identifying threats to our physical well-being. There are basically two parts to threat appraisal – threat detection and threat interpretation. **Threat detection** is usually considered an automatic brain process, meaning the brain is wired to unconsciously scan the environment for threats. This ability is considered to be an evolutionary advantage because fast detection of threat helps keep us safe by allowing ample time to respond. **Threat interpretation** involves our analysis of the information gathered through threat detection. For example, you might think you see a bear while walking in the woods – this is immediate threat detection. However, after taking some time to look more closely, you realize this was a false alarm – there is no bear and you appraise the area as being safe. Threat appraisal is often considered to be a controlled process, but it can occur very quickly and outside our awareness as well.

The brain and body are designed to detect and appraise threats to our physical safety. Psychologists have conducted numerous studies that examine and measure this component of the system[2]. What they have found is that the brain's limbic system -- specifically, the amygdala -- is efficiently designed to detect threats to our physical well-being. The human brain can detect threats at incredibly fast rates. For example, researchers have found that people show fear responses to images presented at 30 milliseconds, which is essentially below humans' threshold of perception (i.e., subliminal). When pictures of potentially dangerous animals (ex: spiders; snakes) are subliminally flashed on a computer screen, the body exhibits a mild fear reaction which psychologists can measure. This is a product of evolution – a brain that detects threat immediately in order to respond as quickly as possible.

Threat Reaction
Once a threat has been identified, the brain and body have to react in some way to offer protection. For example, imagine you are in the woods camping, and you see a bear 100 metres away from you. It is safe to say that your brain has now detected a threat! The body must react to this threat for protection. Many readers have probably heard of the term **"fight or flight response."** Well, there is actually one other response that is not always mentioned – **the freeze response**. When an organism (including human beings) is faced with a threat to physical well-being, the body gets ready to either: (1) fight the threat, (2) run away from the threat, or (3) freeze and hope that an act of submission helps avoid an attack.

The body prepares itself to react to a threat by increasing arousal. Specifically, the hormone **cortisol** is released into the bloodstream and the Sympathetic Nervous System gets activated. These physiological changes in the body produce the following effects:

- Heart beats faster
- Increased blood flow to muscles
- Breathing increases
- We get a quick burst of energy
- Our sensitivity to pain is slightly lowered

Basically, the body is doing its best to prepare to take action. The activation of fear is automatic once the brain finds and appraises something as being a threat.

Monitor Damage

While dealing with a threat to our physical well-being, it is very important to know whether we have been injured in some way. Pain is a critical component of the protection process. Without pain, people are at a heightened risk of further physical harm. Examining case records of people who are born without the ability to feel pain highlights just how valuable pain is to our survival[3]. People born without the ability to feel pain suffer more injuries (some fatal) than the average person. For instance, some people with this affliction try to walk on a broken leg because they couldn't feel the pain from the break. Others have suffered burns without knowing. The infection and damage associated with such injuries can lead to extreme disability and death. Fortunately, the majority of us are born with the ability to feel pain. So, the next time we break a bone we'll go the doctor and start the process of repair. When we touch a stove, we pull our hand away before experiencing further damage. Knowing that we are being harmed, or have been harmed is critically important – it allows us to take some course of action to stop being harmed, which then allows us to start the healing process.

Respond to Pain

When people or animals are physically hurt, they are forced to act in a way that prevents further damage and death. This might include attacking the cause of the pain, or it could involve escaping the situation to heal. If it is the latter decision, for example, the first thing we should do is find a safe place where we can avoid additional threats and attacks, and allow our injuries to heal. If you have a broken arm, you must stop using that arm and take care of it in order for it to heal.

Prepare for Future Threats

A physical threat or actual attack affects our future decision-making. We can learn from our experiences in order to maximize our safety. For example, if you were threatened or attacked by a bear in Jellystone National Park, you might then decide to avoid Jellystone National Park. The brain is designed to learn from past experiences to ensure that we avoid future threats. Avoidance of actual threats (ex: bears) or things that are associated with threats (ex: places like Jellystone National Park) is one way of keeping safe. Another way to increase protection is to improve your ability to handle an attack (ex: learn to fight).

The Need for Social Acceptance – Introducing the Social Protection System

The Physical Protection System has a biologically-based purpose: *it maximizes the survival of our genes*. Similar to the need for physical safety, our need to be liked has the exact same evolutionary purpose: to maximize the survival of our genes. While it is obvious how the need for physical safety relates to the survival of genes, it is probably not as clear how the need to be liked accomplishes the same goal.

Let's imagine people living on Earth thousands of years ago. They basically had two options[4]:

1. They could live in relative isolation from others while trying to survive, or
2. They could form relationships with other people and try to survive as a team or group.

The people who chose option #2 were more likely to survive. Working with other people has many survival advantages. For example, it is easier to build shelter, find food, and defend from attacks (from animals or other people) while working as a team. Also, living with other people increases the likelihood of sexual reproduction.

Of course, not everyone who wanted to be part of a group was automatically accepted. A group of people would only want to accept you if you could offer something in return. In other words, you needed to have some skill that would benefit the group (ex: be a good hunter or builder), or at least be likeable and entertaining! If the group had no purpose for you, you would be rejected and forced to survive on your own. Over time, the people who were accepted by others stood a greater chance of surviving, while those who were rejected did not fare as well. As such, the brain and body became evolutionarily designed to establish relationships with others. In other words, we are hard-wired to seek acceptance and avoid rejection.

Now, you might be saying to yourself – this was thousands of years ago. I don't *need* other people to survive anymore. This is true. But you also probably don't have to keep an eye out for snakes and spiders. Evolution is slow. Although society has changed dramatically, our brains haven't quite caught up. Most of us are designed to live in a world that is much more threatening and dangerous than are our current environments. Unfortunately, simply having this information does very little to decrease our biologically based need to be liked. In other words, you cannot say to yourself – "Hey brain, you don't have to worry about being rejected. Even if people don't like us, we'll be OK." It doesn't work that way. The wiring is already in place. I've heard people say that they "don't need to be liked by others" and I've seen articles on the internet purporting to teach you how "not to need to be liked" and how "not to feel the pain of rejection." These ideas are simply false. We are *built to fear rejection* and *seek acceptance*. The need to be liked is engrained in us, whether we like it or not.

One of the more fascinating aspects of the need to be liked is its relationship to the need for physical safety. The manner in which people strive to be likeable, form relationships and avoid rejection parallels their efforts to be safe and to avoid physical harm. Indeed, based on recent advances in neuropsychological research, it has become clear that the need for safety and the need to be liked share a number of common features, including pain. In fact, research on what psychologists call social pain in humans is what sparked my initial theorizing about how the need to be liked affected people's thoughts, feelings, behaviour, and personality. It was this neuropsychological research, in conjunction with other existing research from the fields of social, cognitive, and clinical psychology that helped me to better understand the many issues my clients were facing in therapy. Indeed, from this point forward, the material presented represents my efforts to synthesize and integrate modern advances in psychological research, contemporary clinical psychology theories, and my own clinical experience.

Before introducing what can be called the *Social Protection System*, it is important to first examine the concept of social pain. **Social pain** refers to the unpleasant feeling people experience following rejection. Some readers might be wondering if I am using the term *pain* in a metaphorical manner. The answer is yes and no. One of the more recent and fascinating findings in the field of neuropsychology is that interpersonal rejection causes responses in the brain that are highly similar to those that occur following physical injury[5]. In other words, the pain of rejection is very real and similar to processes associated with physical pain (described in greater detail below). However, unlike physical pain, there is no site on the body where the pain is specifically felt by the person. Nevertheless, the overall experience of rejection is that it "hurts."

It is also important that I define rejection, as it can have different meanings for different people. Rejection is actually a fairly difficult concept to define, even for psychologists. If your friends haven't called you in weeks, is this rejection? If someone cheats on you, is this an act of rejection? What does it mean if we say that objectively, these are not acts of rejection, yet people *feel* rejected in these cases?

In the end, it is necessary to acknowledge both objective and subjective aspects of rejection.

Rejection can be defined as the act of minimizing the value of a relationship with another person[6]. This definition is a bit abstract, so please allow me to elaborate. When I say "minimize the value of a relationship," it is in reference to our value of the relationship at that time. In other words, if Julie does something that indicates to Mike that she cares less about the relationship than Mike, it is considered a form of rejection. For example, if someone asks us for a divorce, or if someone turns down our request for a date, they are clearly indicating that they value the relationship to a lesser degree than we do. Another more subtle example of rejection would be if your spouse refuses an act of affection (ex: hug or kiss), or when a friend doesn't return your phone call. These are also instances where people are acting as if they value the relationship less than you do (even if it is a temporary devaluation).

Perhaps a simpler way to understand rejection is to use a metaphor. People sometimes use the metaphor of physical distance when discussing how connected they feel to another person. You might say you and your spouse are "close," that a loved one seems "distant" lately, or that a friend appears to be "pushing you away." Whenever someone puts more distance (in terms of level of connection) between themselves and another person, it can be considered an act of rejection.

Objectively speaking, it is possible to say that an act of rejection has or has not occurred according this definition. Our lives are filled with acts of rejection that range from minor (ex: declining to have coffee with a friend) to major (ex: a divorce). There are various factors that determine the amount of pain (if any) from such acts of rejection. Nevertheless, acts of rejection do occur and it is possible to categorize their occurrence.

One of the major problems with defining rejection is that someone could feel incredibly hurt and rejected, even when no act of rejection has technically occurred. For example, if Julie decides to spend the evening with her friends and Mike believes that she is simply trying to "get away from him," then Mike will feel rejected and hurt. In this example, Julie could love Mike and feel completely connected with him. She simply is choosing to spend time with friends, which says nothing about the value of her relationship with Mike. However, Mike's interpretation of Julie's behaviour is what causes him to feel rejected.

In order for rejection to cause pain, you must believe that another person is devaluing your relationship with them or pushing you away. Thus, it is technically possible to feel rejected without an actual occurrence of rejection (objectively speaking). Furthermore, it is also possible to perceive an act of rejection and feel little to no pain. Imagine if you ask someone to go on a date, and they say "no thanks." But then you discover that the reason for the rejection is because the other person is married. This example highlights one of the most important factors that determine the amount of pain felt following a rejection – one's interpretation of *why* they've been rejected.

When somebody believes that a rejection has occurred because of some negative quality they possess (ex: they are rejected because they are unattractive or unpopular), it will be more painful than being rejected for something that has little to do you. For example, if Julie believes that Mike is not giving her affection because he finds her unattractive, then Julie will feel hurt. Conversely, if Julie believes Mike is not giving her affection solely because of a personality trait he possesses (ex: she knows he is not comfortable with affection), then the pain will likely be less intense.

Another factor that determines the pain severity of rejection is the degree to which the relationship is valued by the person being rejected. If someone you don't really

14

care about turns you down, it will hurt much less (or not at all) than if the relationship was very important to you. Therefore, divorces tend to cause more pain than being turned down by strangers (not surprisingly).

The following is a list of examples of rejection in order to help the reader better understand and recognize acts of rejection in daily life:

- Asking a co-worker to have a beer after work and being turned down.

- Having a friend or romantic partner not return your call for a few days (this is subjective because the friend or romantic partner may not actually be devaluing the relationship – ex: perhaps they have been sick).

- Being picked last in a team sport (In this example, the relationship that is being minimized in value is that between the person and the group. In other words, the group is saying – it's not as important for you to be with us).

- Having a stranger get on an otherwise empty bus and not sit anywhere near you (Again, it is important to remember that rejection is about perception, and some people could see rejection in this scenario – ex: they think I look "weird").

It is now time to examine the Social Protection System. The similarities between the Physical Protection System and Social Protection System are quite striking. The evidence presented here is also compelling support for the evolutionary theory of needing to be liked.

The following are the components of the Social Protection System. A direct comparison between the two systems is offered in **Table 1**:

Threat Appraisal

Similar to the Physical Protection System, the Social Protection System includes a threat appraisal component. Specifically, the brain is wired to detect the emotional expressions of other people, including cues of social rejection. The threat detection component of the Social Protection System is similar to its counterpart in the Physical Protection System. For example, similar to the research on detection of physical threat, which shows that people have biased attention toward threats in the environment, researchers have also tested whether people have biased attention for rejection. There are various ways to detect rejection, ranging from the obvious (ex: a person telling you they no longer wish to maintain a relationship with you) to the more subtle and ambiguous (ex: a facial expression or other nonverbal gesture indicating displeasure with you). The efficiency of the brain's ability to detect rejection is highlighted by research on people's ability to detect emotions in others' faces. Knowing whether another person is happy, angry or disgusted can be very useful. It gives us information about other people and their attitudes toward us – including whether we are liked or disliked. On average, the human brain can detect the emotional expression of another person in 80 milliseconds[7]. Our brains pay attention to the emotional expressions of other people, especially when they might indicate rejection of some sort. In addition to emotional expressions, rejection can be detected through other channels, including tone of voice, nonverbal gestures, and the actions of other people. People who are highly sensitive to rejection will detect possible rejection more quickly than those who are not as sensitive (see Chapter 3).

Threat detection is just one aspect of the threat appraisal process. The more critical component of this process is threat interpretation. Threat interpretation refers to the process of deciding whether to "officially" consider something as threatening. Threat interpretations often cause problems for people because of biases in their beliefs (see Chapter 3) and ambiguity in social situations. People pay attention to more than just faces when it comes to detecting rejection. They examine other people's behaviours and words, each of which can range from obvious to ambiguous. Examples include a friend who does not return your call right away, or if someone chooses to sit two seats over from you on a bus. Each of these behaviours can be interpreted as signs of rejection (rightly or wrongly). Thus, relative to physical threat cues, things can get a bit more complicated with rejection cues because of the ambiguity involved.

Respond to Threat

The body's ability to detect physical threat is very similar to its ability to detect social threat. Is there a similarity in physiological arousal as well? In other words, do we experience a fight, flight or freeze response when faced with rejection? The answer appears to be yes. When people fear they might be rejected, they exhibit many of the same responses as when they fear they will be physically harmed. Namely, the body releases cortisol and activates the Sympathetic Nervous System[8].

Have you ever had to speak in public? This is a great example of the similarities between the Physical and Social Protection Systems. More often than not, people experience some level of anxiety before and during a public speech (some more than others). Typically, the moments right before the speech, and during the first 30 seconds or so, the body acts as if it is under attack. Your heart rate and breathing increase, your hands might be shaky, and the muscles are tight. People with a lot of public speaking anxiety can have many more symptoms than this, but these are some of the more common ones. Why in the world do people's bodies react as if they have just seen a bear? Well, when giving a public speech, there is a threat present – maybe the quality of your speech will be poor. How would that affect other people's opinion of you? If they develop a negative opinion of you based on your speech, then this would be a threat of rejection.

Unfortunately for people who have a heightened fear of public speaking, their brain continues to monitor for threat while they are anxiously giving their speech. These people are more likely to (1) identify and pay attention to negative faces in the crowd, and (2) interpret ambiguous faces as being negative[9]. This latter finding highlights the complex nature of the Social Protection System – it will sometimes overreact to possible, but unconfirmed threats (I'll elaborate on this later).

There are many other examples outside of public speaking that highlight anxious bodily reactions in response to potential rejection. Meeting someone for the first time, parties, being on a date, job interviews, and even sending emails, are just some of the many socially-related situations that can cause hearts rates to increase and muscles to tighten.

Monitor Damage

With the *Physical Protection System*, we have feedback from the body about any damage incurred during an attack -- pain. Well, a similar form of feedback is available following perceived instances of rejection. As defined earlier, social pain is what we feel after we've been rejected. It is a feeling that is quite universal. The universal connection between physical pain and rejection is evident in the major languages of the world. These various languages describe being rejected in strikingly similar terms – it is always pain-related. For example, here are some of the common words used in various languages to describe the emotion caused by rejection[10]:

- verletzt sein – a German word meaning "hurt" or "wounded"
- blessé -- French word meaning "hurt"
- gekwetst – a Dutch word meaning "hurt"
- sentirse herido – Spanish for "feeling injured or harmed"
- ferito – Italian word meaning "hurt"
- pligomenos – the Greek word for "hurt"
- megsertoedni – Hungarian expression for being hurt

Thus, over the course of time, these disparate cultural groups all developed words that shared the same meaning when describing the experience of being rejected – "it hurts!"

The difference between social pain and physical pain is obvious: physical pain is caused by broken bones, while social pain is caused by broken hearts (metaphorically speaking). However, research over the past 10-15 years has really opened the eyes of psychologists, as we have learned just how closely intertwined these two systems are. Social pain and physical pain are processed in very similar ways, sometimes using the exact same areas of the brain[11].

For instance, areas of the brain that are responsible for processing physical pain are identical to those that process social pain. Specifically, the Anterior Cingulate Cortex (ACC) and the Periaqueductal Gray (PAG) receive and process information about physical pain when the body is injured. Similarly, these areas of the brain also become activated and process information when someone is rejected. For example, when you measure brain activity (ex: with an fMRI) while someone is being rejected, the brain responds as if the person had just been physically injured. In this way, it can literally hurt to have your heart broken. To our brains, pain is pain – plain and simple.

If being rejected by someone causes pain via certain brain structures, then we should see deactivation of these structures when the opposite happens – namely, when people accept us in some way. Researchers have recently demonstrated such a finding[12]. When research subjects were rejected, but then offered social support, the ACC in their brain became activated (causing pain during rejection), and then deactivated during emotional support. This type of research really highlights the impact that we have on each other. If you reject your friend, you cause activation of a part of their brain which will cause pain, and if you support a rejected friend, you deactivate this same area of the brain, which is soothing.

Further evidence linking social and physical pain comes from animal research. Basic research involving animals is valuable because their bodies operate similarly to our own. Animal research has shown that animals' bodies respond to social pain similarly to physical pain. Specifically, when rats are kept in social isolation from other rats, their bodies release hormones called opioids. Opioids are commonly produced in animals and humans in response to physical pain because they serve an analgesic function (i.e., they reduce pain). It is therefore quite interesting that the neuroendocrine system of socially isolated animals produces these hormones.

Both social and physical pain are also significantly associated with unpleasant emotions, such as depression, anxiety and fear. In other words, you see very similar emotional responses to pain – regardless of whether the pain is physical or social in origin. In fact, the extremes of each type of pain really highlight this relationship. For example, individuals with a chronic form of either pain (chronic pain or prolonged social isolation) are especially likely to feel depressed.

Overall, researchers are learning more and more about the fascinating connection between social pain and physical pain. What is even more interesting is that both types of pain seem to serve similar functions – they offer feedback that is (or was) important to survival. Physical pain is useful because it lets us know of an injury, and allows us to respond accordingly. Similarly, social pain makes us aware of a problem (ex: problems with relationships), which allows us to respond accordingly.

Respond to Damage
When you've been physically injured, one way to protect yourself is to attack the cause of the injury, or avoid additional injuries by running away and finding a place

to heal. Similar responses occur among people who have been rejected – particularly if the rejection caused a high degree of pain. A common emotional reaction to the pain of rejection is anger. Results from correlational and experimental studies show a very strong tendency for people to get angry and take action against the offending party[13]. For example, people who feel rejected are more likely to criticize and derogate the person who rejected them. In fact, rejection can sometimes lead to violence. A common cause of murder in marriages is an act of rejection, and social isolation is considered a greater causal factor in youth violence than is gang membership.

However, anger, criticism and violence are not the only responses to rejection. Following a significant rejection experience, people sometimes also get sad – even depressed. When people become depressed, one of the things that psychologists often see is withdrawal from other people – it is like a form of self-imposed alienation. This makes sense from the perspective that the person is trying to avoid additional pain. This is similar to the "flight" response you might use following physical injury. By keeping a distance from people, you are essentially protecting yourself while in a vulnerable state (ex: don't let anyone else reject you)[14].

In terms of healing, people who have been rejected will often turn to others for support. So, talking to a friend or family member, or a mental health professional are options that many people exercise. As noted above, when we receive support from other people, it helps to ease social pain by deactivating pain centres in the brain. It is interesting to note that emotional support can also ease physical pain as well. For example, researchers have found that pain thresholds increase (ex: people can keep their hand in a bucket of ice water for longer periods of time) when someone is standing next to them and offering support[15]. I hope readers are really getting a good sense of how closely connected the social and physical pain systems are to each other.

21

Another method of self-healing that people with depression use is searching for the cause of rejection. Gaining insight into what transpired in the past can be therapeutic in at least two ways: (1) understanding what happened could lead to a different interpretation of the rejection (ex: the relationship did not end because of problems with me – there are other factors at play), and (2) if the person is able to identify a trait or quality about themselves that helped cause the rejection, they can then fix this problem, thereby offering hope for future relationships.

Indeed, people with depression often try to accomplish these goals – albeit, not always with a lot of success. First, people with depression become more ruminative than usual, and more than people without depression[16]. When people ruminate they spend a lot of time thinking about themselves, their depression, and things that have happened in the past. Psychologists presume that this pattern of thought occurs, at least in part, to try and find meaning and understanding.

Second, people with depression are also more likely to engage in self-criticism. Self-criticism occurs when people try to identify flaws in order to make improvements to oneself, as a way of becoming more appealing to others. For example, if people tend to reject you because you are overly aggressive, this is a quality that could be changed to improve the likelihood of being accepted in the future.

People with depression or even mild levels of sadness engage in these types of attempted healing processes. Sometimes these processes can be helpful. However, they are oftentimes unhelpful, and can magnify feelings of sadness and depression. I will elaborate on these issues, and how to correct them in later chapters. For the time being, it is important to note that social pain seems to cause an emotional reaction (sadness/ depression) that leads people to seek safety and attempt to heal their pain.

22

Prepare for Future Threats

When someone has been rejected and has experienced significant social pain, they are likely changed in some way from their experience. They may have taken the time to try and understand what has happened in order to prevent such an experience from occurring again. Remember, the goal is to be liked by other people so we can form relationships. This is why we have a feedback system -- it enables us to identify problems with likeability and make appropriate changes. For example, if you have relationship problems because you are too "clingy" or "overly sensitive to criticism," then identifying these problems and making changes is a useful process.

Unfortunately, this process can be complicated by mistakes made in the previous steps of the Social Protection System. For example, some people try and make changes when none are necessary. I will use a case vignette to explain this point:

> *Kim is a 22 year-old college student. She has had 2 serious relationships in the past 2 years. Kim ended the first relationship after she learned that her boyfriend cheated on her. The second relationship was terminated by her boyfriend of 10 months. He told her that he did not think they were "a good match." Kim, who was average in weight, began dieting soon after the second relationship ended. She felt compelled to improve her appearance by being thinner.*

Many people would sympathize with Kim. I mean, who would want to be rejected in multiple relationships? Kim has decided to prevent such rejections from occurring again by changing some aspect of herself. The logic here is that by becoming more attractive, it will make rejection more difficult in the future. However, an important question for Kim to ask is "was I rejected because I am unlikeable to other people (to men?)?" And also "was my appearance the reason for my unlikeability?"

Thus, a proper understanding of the rejection is important before moving forward with this stage (i.e., preparing for future threats). It is especially important to determine whether there is something truly unlikeable and unacceptable about you. It is one thing to believe that someone does not like you. Most people can live with this fact. It is a completely different thing when you feel you are not likeable as a person. When you feel there is some kind of defect that others can or will see (sooner or later), which has the inevitable consequence of causing rejection, it can make you feel depressed and hopeless. Personally, I completely sympathize with people when they become depressed in this way. I mean, if I actually believed that I was generally unlikeable, and that most future relationships would either (1) not be possible because people would not want to enter into a relationship with me, or (2) eventually end because the other person would realize how unlikeable I am – I would be depressed as well.

In this case, Kim's reaction (trying to make herself more attractive) is actually in some ways a logical move. She believes on some level (either consciously or unconsciously – we'll get to this later), that she is unlikeable and that this is the reason for her rejection. Therefore, it is important to prevent future rejection. The problem with Kim's approach is that her "theory" as to why she was rejected is wrong, yet she is taking significant steps change herself. Unfortunately, the changes are unnecessary.

Concluding Comments on the Social Protection System

There are 3 components of the Social Protection System that we have some control over – threat appraisal, response to rejection, and preparation for future threat. The other two (threat detection and pain detection) are primarily automatic, physiological reactions, and are essentially beyond our control (assuming there is no use of medication, alcohol or drugs). These 3 components shape much of your life in ways that you are probably only vaguely aware of. For example, similar to Kim's reaction, people sometimes make changes to themselves that are not necessary, and they may not even be aware why they have chosen to do so.

The Social Protection System, as it has been presented here, is not a serial process system. This means that people do not necessarily move from one level to the other in a neat and orderly fashion. There is some overlap among the stages, and they often interact to some degree. For instance, threat appraisal is often ongoing across all other levels, so that even if you are depressed and "healing," your brain may still be aware of threats of rejection. Furthermore, some of the activities that occur at the Response to Damage stage also occur during the Preparation for Future Threat stage. For example, you might be making changes to your behaviour, yet still engaging in self-critical thinking. It is best to consider the Social Protection System as a general framework, which can be used to help conceptualize and understand various psychological reactions and processes.

There are many reasons to try and be liked by other people. The attention feels good, as does the security of being in relationships. Being with people brings all kinds of opportunities for reward and pleasure, such as having fun at parties, enjoyable conversations, sharing food, sexual pleasure, physical protection, benefits of reciprocity, etc. However, as demonstrated by the Social Protection System, being liked by others and being a likeable person makes it less likely to feel social pain. Pain is an incredibly motivating experience. The remainder of this book focuses primarily on how both actual pain and the threat of pain motivate people to think and behave in particular ways, with a particular emphasis on how this process can be dysfunctional.

Readers can see an overview of these systems in the table below. As discussed, both systems are very similar. In fact, watching someone react to social threats can look almost identical to watching the same person react to physical threats. Examining the similarities in these systems helps explain our need for social acceptance.

Table 1. *Comparing the Physical and Social Protection Systems*

	Physical Protection System	Social Protection System
Goal	Keep the person alive to increase probability of gene survival.	Form relationships with people to increase probability of gene survival.
Threat Appraisal	Brain is wired to detect and appraise threats to physical well-being.	Brain is wired to detect and appraise threats to social well-being.
Threat Reaction	Body is prepared for action by releasing cortisol and activating the Sympathetic Nervous System.	Body is prepared for action by releasing cortisol and activating the Sympathetic Nervous System.
Monitor Damage	Pain indicates a threat to the main goal of safety.	Pain indicates a threat to main goal of being liked by others..
Respond to Damage	React to the attack and take time to heal.	React to the rejection and take time to heal.
Prepare for the Future	Use learning experiences to prevent harm in the future. For example, you could avoid dangerous places or become a better fighter.	Use learning experiences to avoid the pain of rejection in the future. For example, you can avoid intimate relationships or improve how likeable you are to other people.

Chapter 3

CORE BELIEFS AND PROBLEMS WITH THREAT APPRAISAL

At this point, I hope the importance of being liked has become clearer. We were designed through evolution to form relationships with other people, so being liked and accepted is a natural part of life. The consequence of failing to be liked by others is the feeling of pain, not to mention other negative emotions, such as sadness and anxiety. Avoidance of pain is not the only motivating factor behind relationship formation, as there are many other positive factors that draw us to connect with people. Nevertheless, the threat of pain from rejection is powerful, and is responsible for shaping much of our behaviour.

In Chapter 2, you learned about the Social Protection System, and about the initial component of this system – threat appraisal. Threat appraisal is a necessary component to both the Physical and Social Protection Systems because it provides very useful information; namely, whether we are at risk of harm. With the physical system, the risk is physical harm and possible death. With the social system, the risk is being disliked and alienated by people. Being unlikeable to others is the threat that we've been wired and designed to avoid. Again, this is an evolutionary design, so it doesn't make complete sense in today's society.

We are not at the mercy of our brain's threat appraisal system. Even if our brains alert us to potential rejection cues (threat detection), we can examine this information and decide either to accept or to reject it (threat interpretation). The same is true of the Physical Protection System. Imagine you are camping and you think you see a bear across the field – your body may start to respond immediately to prepare to act. However, rather than running and assuming you are in danger, you take a second to further consider the threat information. You look a little closer and realize that it is not a bear – just a false alarm (ex: a harmless furry animal). When you recognize that the threat is false, your Parasympathetic System will kick in, and your body will cancel its emergency response. Similarly, when people take the time to examine social information more closely, they too can spot a false alarm. This is not always an easy process, and is often a source of consternation for many people.

Problems with Threat Appraisal

Although people have the ability to re-examine threat detection signals to see if they are accurate, this process can be difficult. Indeed, the ability to examine your thinking and identify false alarms of rejection can be much harder than it sounds – especially for people who are shy, insecure and/ or socially anxious. First, their threat system could be hyperactive – meaning they are able to see threat in many situations – even situations that are quite free of threat.

Second, when it comes to threat interpretation, you are ultimately required to make a decision – "Am I being rejected or not?" Ideally, this decision would be grounded in facts, logic and reality. Unfortunately, people are not always motivated to make such realistic decisions. Rather, they are often motivated to make the safe decision. Allow me to elaborate on both of these problems with threat appraisal.

First, people are not wired to pay attention to all things equally. Our attention is often biased towards threat, and some people have stronger attention biases than others. For instance, imagine that Jim has a fear of dogs. Imagine further that he decides to take a walk in the park with a friend, who does not share his fear of dogs. Who do you think will be the first one to spot a dog? Also, who do you think is more likely to mistake other animals as being dogs? The answer to both questions is Jim.

Because Jim has a greater fear of dogs, he is going to be more vigilant for their presence. Also, because his brain is always unconsciously scanning the environment for dogs, it is more likely to have false positives – mistaking other animals (ex: cats) as being dogs. Similarly, people with a greater fear of rejection are going to (1) detect possible rejection more quickly, and (2) experience more false-positives, by seeing rejection where there is none. When your attention is biased in this manner, it can be extra difficult to examine your thoughts to determine if rejection has actually occurred. Someone who is very sensitive to rejection is highly motivated to avoid the pain of rejection. Therefore, they are going to try and spot rejection as quickly as possible in order to take immediate action.

Even if someone with a strong fear of rejection experiences a false positive (i.e., they interpret someone else's behaviour as indicating rejection when this is not the case), they should be able to correct for this mistake if there is evidence to the contrary. For example, imagine you are on a date and the other person cuts the evening short because he/ she feels ill. You quickly assume that this is an excuse to avoid spending any more time together. However, imagine that the date calls you back the next day and says he/she is feeling better. Furthermore, they ask to go on another date this weekend. In this situation, there was a false-positive (you assumed there was rejection, which was not true), and you were able to eventually correct for this mistake when there was obvious information to the contrary (when the other person asked you out again). It would have been possible (and healthier) to avoid feeling rejected sooner if you hadn't jumped to conclusions.

Unfortunately, social encounters do not always provide us with such clear-cut information (like a phone call). Many situations involve ambiguity. So, what happens when there is ambiguous rejection information? Do you assume you have been rejected, or pretend as though nothing has happened? Two people can be faced with identical information, and yet have two completely different reactions. This is true for both the Physical and Social Protection systems. Using the Physical Protection System as an example, imagine that two people notice pains in their chest. This is potential threat information. It could be a heart attack, or it could be heart-burn. Someone who is very anxious might decide to visit the ER immediately. A less anxious person is more likely to consider other information before making a decision (ex: what did I eat today? Are there other heart attack symptoms that support this possibility?). The point here is that people can differ drastically in terms of their **motivation** when facing ambiguous information. Some people are motivated to make the safest possible decision, while others are motivated to make the most realistic/ logical explanation. I will use an example to explain this process further.

Imagine there are two people – Mark and Tom. Based on his experiences in life, Mark is fairly certain that he is likeable to others. Tom is much more uncertain of himself. He hopes that other people like him, but for the most part he is unsure if this is actually the case. Imagine that both Mark and Tom decide to ask someone from work to have a beer with them after their shift has ended. In both cases, the co-worker says that he or she is too busy, and suggests they do it another time. This could be rejection – the co-worker could be making an excuse not to spend time with them. Mark and Tom both have access to the same information -- they cannot be certain that their co-worker likes them. They have two choices at this point.

First, they can assume that everything is OK, and that a rejection has not occurred. Choosing this option seems like a relatively safe choice. By assuming there has been no rejection, you get to avoid the pain of rejection. However, there is a consequence to this choice. If you make this choice, you are deciding that the other steps in the Social Protection System are not required. There is no need to protect yourself from further rejection, no need to assess what has happened, and no need to make any changes to prevent future rejection. In other words, by choosing to ignore the possibility of rejection, you could be opening yourself up to more harm in the long run. Remember, both the Physical and Social Protection Systems serve a purpose. If you ignore actual threats, you could be leaving yourself open to consequences in the future.

The second option here is to assume that you have been rejected. You can then act accordingly (ex: avoid asking that person to do something again; try and figure out why they might not like you). Thus, the second option is, from the standpoint of the Social Protection System, the *safer* option for Tom. Examine **Table 2** to understand Tom's decision-making process in this situation.

Table 2. *The Rejection Dilemma*

	You were truly rejected	**You were not rejected**
Choice #1 **Assume rejection**	Vulnerable, but taking action to protect self	Safe, but taking action to protect self
Choice #2 **Assume no rejection**	Vulnerable	Safe

As outlined in the **Rejection Dilemma Table**, there are four consequences, depending on the assumptions you make and the reality of the situation. Notice that the top two columns are unknown to the person – the situation involves ambiguity, and so you cannot be certain if there has or has not been rejection. The two rows represent your choices – you can assume there's been rejection or ignore this possibility. This results in four potential outcomes. Choice #1 is the "safest" because it leads to self-protection. Choice #2 is technically the "riskiest" because there is the potential for vulnerability.

When Tom assumes that he has been rejected, he can then take action to protect himself. Conversely, if he assumes there was no rejection, there is a chance he might be vulnerable to future rejections. Specifically, if Tom assumes he has not been rejected, then he could be ignoring an actual threat. For example, he might ask the person to hang out again prompting another rejection. Alternatively, there could be something unlikeable about Tom that is causing the rejection, which ideally should be identified to prevent future rejections. In general, when unsure if you have been rejected, assuming you have been rejected is the safest option because it leads to protective action. Technically speaking, this is also the safest option for Mark as well, but he has decided that the consequences are too minimal. Allow me to elaborate on this latter point a bit further.

Every time we are faced with a possible rejection, we could follow all the steps of the Social Protection System. We could assume we've been rejected (regardless of the information), feel some pain, which then motivates us to protect ourselves, figure out what is going on and make appropriate changes. Doing this would help ensure that we are likeable to other people. This would also be exhausting. It would be akin to running to the doctor every time you noticed a physical symptom. Technically speaking, it might provide the most protection from harm, but it is both inefficient and impractical.

The more efficient option is to evaluate each threat and determine if it merits additional attention. If someone rejects you, this does not mean you are unlikeable or unacceptable. You need more information to make a decision. First of all, how well does this person know you? A relative stranger is going to provide less pertinent information about your likeability relative to a close friend or spouse. Second, is this an isolated incident or a trend? Generally speaking, what kind of information are you getting from people?

For Mark, he decided that no further action was needed. Even if he was wrong – that he was actually being rejected – the consequences are minimal. This is a stranger and only one person. Tom could have made the exact same decision, but he felt compelled to make the safe choice, which was to protect himself from further pain down the road. I hope this helps to highlight an important point – people who are confident often don't feel compelled to make the safe choice – they try and make the *realistic* choice. The reasons why Tom and Mark made these different choices will be reviewed below in the section on core beliefs.

To quickly sum up, the threat appraisal system is not always reality-based or accurate. For some people, their ability to detect rejection will be much faster than others. But this speed has a trade-off; specifically, there will be more errors in spotting rejection. Furthermore, people who are very sensitive to rejection are oftentimes more motivated to make the safe choice. As a consequence, they will assume rejection in ambiguous situations in order to maximize self-protection.

An important question now arises – what determines things like threat detection threshold, level of rejection sensitivity, and feelings of confidence and insecurity? Let's talk about core beliefs.

An Introduction to Core Beliefs

When we are born, we are not clean slates. There are genetic factors that play a significant role in our development, including the development of our personality. However, research shows that we do a fair amount of learning throughout our lives. And this learning, or life experience, plays a very significant role in determining the type of people we become. From an evolutionary perspective, the ability to learn allows us to adapt to the environment around us. For example, if you are born and raised in a violent part of the world (ex: Baghdad, Iraq), it is important that you see the world differently than someone born in a very safe part of the world (ex: Ottawa, Canada). It is important that the child born in Iraq learns to be more vigilant for threat and violence. He has to be less trusting of people and places than his counterpart in Ottawa – for the sake of survival.

Throughout our experiences in life, we all come to form beliefs in our mind about the world, other people and ourselves[17]. If you are born and raised in Baghdad, you are more likely to believe:

1.   The world is a dangerous place,

2.   Strangers are likely to be dangerous and must be trusted with caution, and

3.   You are fairly vulnerable to harm

I am not saying everyone in Baghdad thinks this way, only that you are more likely to form these beliefs from your experiences there, relative to the average person raised in Ottawa. I hope it is clear why it is necessary to form beliefs that closely match the world you live in – it facilitates adaption to that environment.

When it comes to social beliefs, the process operates essentially the same way. The environment in which we are raised, and our experiences therein, largely determine our beliefs. If you are raised in a home with physical violence, you may come to believe that:

1.   People cannot always be trusted, and

2. I am relatively worthless. I am worthless because my parents abused me, while other children's parents loved them – therefore, I must have less value than other people.

Again, these are just some of the possible beliefs that could develop in such an environment. In fact, it makes sense that we develop thinking styles that mirror our upbringing. For many children and adolescents raised in these kinds of environments, the development of these beliefs helps keep them safe. They allow us to adapt to the world we know. **Core beliefs** are general principles that guide our behaviour. They are the products of our life experiences. Everything that happens in life gets filtered through these beliefs. Furthermore, each belief will have corresponding rules of behaviour. For example, if you hold the core belief "people are usually selfish and untrustworthy" the corresponding rule will likely be "act cautiously in relationships."

Although there are general rules associated with each core belief, there can be exceptions to these rules. Just because you have a core belief that other people cannot be trusted easily, does not guarantee you will never trust anybody. Under the right conditions, you could trust somebody special, yet still hold the core belief that people, generally speaking, cannot be trusted. There can be exceptions to the rules we create, but the rules are still there.

We can form core beliefs about many things. However, not all core beliefs will significantly affect our lives. Some of the more significant core beliefs in existence are the ones I mentioned earlier – beliefs about the world (or your immediate environment), other people and yourself. You can tell a lot about a person based on these three core beliefs. For example, imagine that someone believes the following:

1. The world is dangerous,

2. Other people cannot be trusted, and

3.   I am vulnerable to death and harm most of the time

This person is probably going to be quite anxious. Now imagine that another person believes that:

1.   The world is full of pain and heart-ache

2.   People don't really care about me

3.   For the most part, I am unlikeable to other people.

This person is likely to feel depressed because of these beliefs.

The core beliefs that are most relevant to the current topic of needing to be liked are #s 2 and 3 – our core beliefs of other people and ourselves. These core beliefs play a very significant role in determining how the Social Protection System operates. Specifically, these core beliefs will significantly affect threat appraisal, response to damage, and preparation for future threat. However, before discussing how core beliefs affect the functioning of the Social Protection System, I am going to briefly elaborate on the functioning of core beliefs.

Core beliefs and Everyday Thinking

I would venture to say that most people are not always aware of their core beliefs. In fact, people are not always aware of many of the brain's thought processes. The past 20 years or so of psychological research has really shed light on how the brain processes information. It appears that there are two primary types of thinking – automatic thinking and controlled thinking[18]. **Controlled thinking** is deliberate and intentional. It is pretty much under your control. For example, if you wanted to list your favourite movies, you could think about it and give an answer. Also, if someone asked you to describe your personality, you could take the time to deliberate and provide a response. Controlled thinking is intentional and manipulated by the person.

Automatic thinking occurs without our intention or motivation, and it will often occur without awareness. To help explain this type of thinking further, let me offer an example:

> *Imagine you see a spider scurry across your kitchen floor. It's a tiny spider that is obviously quite harmless. Yet, you take a step back and feel a bit anxious. You might think "I hate spiders!" However, if someone asked you if the spider was harmful or dangerous, you'd probably say "no -- I know it's not harmful, but I just don't like them." What's going on here?*

Psychologists believe that automatic thinking is based on **associative connections in the brain**. An associative connection is a neural link between two concepts or ideas. For example, you are likely to think of the word "eggs" when someone says "bacon and _____." Why? Because eggs and bacon are often paired together -- in meals and in sentences or expressions. So, over time we associate these two things together. In fact, we could create a whole network of associations. For example, eggs, bacon, toast and coffee are more likely to be associated than things like car and grass. This means that thinking of one thing (ex: bacon) makes it more likely for something related to come to mind (ex: eggs or toast).

People build associative networks for all kinds of things -- like spiders, for example. Throughout your life, spiders have probably been associated with more bad than good. You might have seen your mother jump in fear at the sight of a spider. You might have watched a show on the *Discovery Network* showing spiders trap, kill and eat insects. You've probably heard how some spiders are deadly. In any case, most people make connections between spiders and negative things. Therefore, it is common for people to have at least a little bit of fear or discomfort when seeing a spider. When you see a spider, it activates negative associations and we're often left with a *negative feeling* of some sort -- a discomfort or feeling of anxiety.

So, to review how automatic thinking works:

1.   A network of associations is created in the brain,

2.   These associations become "activated" (similar to turning on electricity)

3.   The activation of a network of associations can cause emotional reactions and certain thoughts to come to mind.

People are often only aware of the emotions or thoughts at the end of this process. The creation and activation of the network is automatic and usually outside of the person's awareness -- hence, it can be considered unconscious processing or unconscious thinking.

Notice too that these networks can lead us to form beliefs. In the spider example I just used, the person (let's call him Ben) might have the belief "I hate spiders" based on this network in the brain. Based on his "spider experiences" in life, Ben has formed a core belief ("I hate spiders"). This core belief will make certain thoughts ("Man, I really don't like spiders"), emotions (ex: anxiety; disgust), and behaviours (ex: avoiding pet stores at the mall) more likely to occur for Ben. Although he logically knows that most spiders are not harmful, the automatic nature of his *spider network* in the brain significantly influences his psychological reactions.

In addition to a spider network and spider core beliefs, Ben will also have other networks in the brain. He will have networks for things like social events and people. He will even have a network that is dedicated solely to *the self*. In other words, Ben's self-concept, or his understanding of who he is as a person will be based on a network of associations that have accumulated over the course of his life. This network will include core beliefs and will guide his thinking, emotional reactions and behaviour.

Like spiders, we can create a network of associations to *ourselves* through life experiences. Imagine Ben having repeated failure experiences while growing up. Perhaps he was a poor student and his father, teachers and peers criticized and mocked his struggles (ex: "You're so stupid"). For Ben, each of these experiences got paired with the concept of "me." And over time, the concept of failure and the memories of these experiences become an engrained part of his *self network*. This self network leads to the creation of a core belief – in this case, "I am a failure" or "I am stupid."

In addition to the creation of core beliefs, self networks are also responsible for automatic thinking. Anyone who has ever purchased a book on Cognitive Behaviour Therapy (CBT) has likely read the expression **automatic thoughts**. These thoughts are often a focal point of psychological treatment because (1) they affect our emotions, and (2) people often don't notice them or challenge them. For example, if you had the core belief of being a "failure" and you walk into a classroom to write an exam, you might only be aware of certain emotions (ex: anxiety; hopelessness). Not everyone in this situation is aware of the thoughts going through their mind as well. Thoughts such as "why can I never get anything right?" and "I'm definitely going to fail this test" are examples of automatic thinking. The self network has been activated and you are viewing everything through your *Failure* core belief (like a filter). It is causing all kinds of negative thoughts and predictions to occur, which are in turn causing unpleasant emotions. Interestingly, people in this situation may only be aware of the emotions themselves, and little else.

Levels of psychological awareness vary from person to person. Someone can be aware of (1) a core belief, (2) the situations where this core belief is likely to affect thinking, (3) the automatic thoughts that come to mind in these situations, and (4) the subsequent emotions. However, awareness of these things varies considerably. I have had clients with full awareness, some awareness, and no awareness (not even the emotions being felt).

Before we move forward, let's summarize:

1.   In order to learn from our life experiences, the brain creates networks of information. These networks allow us to form general beliefs – also called core beliefs.

2.   There can be a network of the self, and therefore we can form core beliefs of the self (ex: "I am incompetent" and "I am unlikeable"). There can also be networks about other people and relationships (ex: "People are untrustworthy" and "Relationships are painful").

3.   These networks and their associated core beliefs affect the thoughts we have. In fact, our core beliefs can cause what psychologists call **automatic thoughts**. These are thoughts that go through our mind in given situations, with or without us being aware of them.

4.   The automatic thoughts we experience affect our emotions.

5.   We are not always aware of this process. We are usually most aware of the emotion(s) we feel at the end.

Core Beliefs and the Social Protection System

To explain how core beliefs affect the Social Protection System, I am going to use the example of Mark and Tom again. Remember, Mark believes he is likeable and feels confident, while Tom is uncertain about his likeability and feels insecure. I am going to add a third person – Lisa. Lisa believes she is unlikeable and feels depressed. The following are brief case histories for these three fictional characters.

Mark

Mark is 26 years-old and works for an IT company. His childhood and adolescence were pretty normal. He tended to make friends well, and formed a few close friendships over the years. Despite some heated arguments with his parents while in high school, Mark maintained good relationships with both his mother and father. Mark dated several people throughout high school and university. In college, Mark had his heart broken after his girlfriend left him following 2 years of dating. However, he eventually recovered and is now dating someone new. Mark continues to hang out with some of his friends from high school, but also has made new friends at work. Overall, Mark is happy and feels confident about himself.

Tom

Tom is 26 years-old and works for an IT company. His childhood and adolescence were fairly normal. However, there are several notable experiences from these early years. First, when Tom was 8 years old he had an argument with his best friend which led to a fist-fight. The next day at school, Tom learned that his friend had spread a nasty rumour about him to the other students. Tom was teased for a few weeks, but eventually the other children forgot about it and Tom made new friends. Second, in high school, Tom's girlfriend at the time cheated on him with one of Tom's friends. Third, Tom has always had a poor relationship with his brother. He could never get along well with his older brother, who often called Tom a "loser" and never wanted to spend time with him. Tom's brother was very popular at school. Finally, while in college, Tom was really hurt when a few of his friends took a road trip and did not invite him. As mentioned, Tom is insecure and unsure of himself and relationships.

Lisa

Lisa is 26 years-old and works for an IT company. She had a complex relationship with her mother. Lisa's mother was in many ways a loving person, but could be very critical at times. In fact, she often made critical remarks about Lisa's weight and appearance. It was as if her mother was somewhat embarrassed by her, and she often encouraged Lisa to exercise or eat healthier snacks. Lisa always had the impression that her mother loved her sister more. Lisa had a great relationship with her sister (Cheryl), who was very attractive and popular at school. However, her mother seemed to prefer her sister in some ways. For example, Lisa's mother often asked Cheryl to go shopping at the mall, but never Lisa. Lisa's dad was also very nice, and they had a great relationship. However, her father often criticized her for not doing well enough in school. Although Lisa was an average student, this did not meet her father's expectations. Lisa made friends very easily for the first 10 years of her life. However, after the family moved to a new town, she had a lot of trouble fitting in at a new school. She was bullied by two of the girls at her new school for over a year. Finally, when Lisa was in her second year of university, she learned that her boyfriend cheated on her several times with 3 other women. Lisa has experienced problems with depression and believes there are serious problems with her likeability.

Based on the information presented in these case histories, it is clear that Mark, Tom and Lisa had different interpersonal experiences. All three of them experienced negative interpersonal events at various points in their lives – some more than others. For Mark, although people have generally liked him, some people have not. Also, he had a girlfriend end their relationship because she no longer wanted to be with him. Yet, Mark's first 26 years of life have taught him that he is, for the most part, a likeable and acceptable person. He has also learned that other people can be trusted.

Tom's experiences have been more ambiguous. There have been a number of times where he has been able to make and maintain friendships. However, there have been a few key moments in his life that have made him second-guess how likeable he is. How could he be confident that he is likeable when his own brother refuses to spend time with him? Why would his friend and girlfriend treat him so poorly? Why would his close buddies choose to exclude him from their trip? Tom has received conflicting information about his likeability, which has affected his core beliefs. He believes that he is somewhat likeable, but once people get to know him, they see something they don't like. In other words, Tom believes there is something defective about him. He has also formed the belief that other people, including friends, should not be given too much trust. These beliefs have caused feelings of insecurity and doubt in relationships.

Lisa's experiences have taught her that she is "not good enough." This makes sense – why else would her parents constantly give her feedback that she is inadequate in some way. Also, why else would she be bullied and why did her boyfriend cheat on her? Clearly, in Lisa's mind, there is something missing. She could be likeable if she could change something – maybe her appearance? But for now, Lisa believes that she is unlikeable and that people can be very hurtful.

The following is a summary of the core beliefs for Mark, Tom and Lisa, and an example of rules based on these beliefs:

Mark
1. I am likeable to most people
2. Other people can be trusted
Rule: If you want to form a relationship with someone, it is generally safe to do so.

Tom
1. There is something defective about me that other people don't like
2. People are unpredictable
Rule: It is OK to form relationships, but don't let people get too close to you.

Lisa

1. I am inadequate the way I am
2. People are often critical and rejecting.

Rule: Be very careful around people. Only show them the positive aspects of yourself to avoid disapproval and rejection.

If you had Mark, Tom and Lisa estimate how vulnerable to rejection they were on a scale from 1 (not at all vulnerable) to 10 (completely vulnerable), they would probably provide the following ratings: Mark (2/10 – low vulnerability), Tom (6/10 – moderate vulnerability) and Lisa (9/10 - high vulnerability). Our core beliefs allow us to make estimations about how vulnerable we are to rejection. This sense of vulnerability plays a primary role in determining how the Social Protection System operates.

Core Beliefs, Vulnerability and the Social Protection System: Putting it all Together

Imagine you are walking down a dirt road through the woods. While walking, you see a sign that says there are bears in the area, so proceed with caution. Now imagine you are driving in an SUV down a dirt road in the same area, and you notice the sign that warns of bears. It's safe to say that you would be more vigilant for bears while walking, because you are more vulnerable. It makes sense for our threat appraisal system to vary in its level of vigilance according to our perceived level of vulnerability. This same principle applies to threat appraisal of rejection.

For many people, socializing and trying to form new relationships with others is like walking through a forest where bears live. There will be caution and anxiety. The person will be scanning the environment for possible threat. What was that sound?

45

Is that person talking about me? Did I see something move in those bushes? Does this person seem annoyed talking to me? The person knows there is potential danger, and so he/ she must take care to protect themselves at all cost. The more vulnerable someone feels, the more they will feel motivated to keep themselves safe. So, their threshold for threat detection will be lower.

To highlight how one's sense of vulnerability to rejection interacts with the Social Protection System, imagine that Lisa is dating someone new. Because she feels very vulnerable to rejection, she will be paying close attention to the other person's actions -- looking for possible signs of rejection (ex: "does he seem annoyed or bored with me"). She is more likely to see rejection when there is none. For example, if he doesn't immediately return her phone call it might mean he is getting tired of being with her. Let's say that her new boyfriend has not returned her phone call from the day before. She believes this is the beginning of the end, and assumes he no longer wants to be with her.

When Lisa is faced with the threat of this rejection, she can fight, flee or freeze. If she "fights" the rejection, she might start to cling to him. For example, going to his house and telling him she loves him, and that she would get very depressed (even suicidal) if they ever broke-up. Alternatively, she could simply run away from the rejection before it happens. For example, she might call him up and break-up with him. Finally, she could do nothing, except feel depressed and helpless and assume the rejection is inevitable. Each of these behaviours actually increases the likelihood of the rejection happening. If she gets clingy or acts depressed and aloof around him, this will have the unfortunate effect of pushing him away. If she breaks up with him first, obviously this would end the relationship directly.

Assume that their relationship ends because of one of these actions. Lisa will then feel the pain of this separation/ rejection. The next steps in the Social Protection

46

System are to respond to this pain (i.e., find a safe place to heal and recover) and prepare for future threats. For many people following a relationship break-up, they often turn to a friend for social support. However, Lisa decides not to do this. She is so hurt that she does not want to be around anyone. She lies in bed and feels depressed. To her, this break-up is more evidence that she is unlikeable to other people. She does not want to talk about her thoughts and feelings to anyone because she will just bother them with her problems and push them away as well. Also, she cannot trust people at this time. What if she tells someone about the relationship and they criticize her and point out how she failed in the relationship? That would be too much pain to handle. Therefore, Lisa lies in bed and ruminates about what happened. She thinks about all her negative qualities and how unlikeable she must be to other people. She thinks that maybe her mother is right – she is unattractive and this is what causes men to leave her. She eventually starts to recover from her depression, but decides that she will lose weight before ever dating again (preparation for future threat).

This example highlights how one's sense of vulnerability and core beliefs can affect decision-making and behaviour. First, before entering the relationship Lisa believed that she was unlikeable and that other people were likely to see her flaws and reject her. Therefore, at the first sign of possible rejection Lisa took action, which had the unfortunate consequence of causing the relationship's demise – a *self-fulfilling prophecy*. Next, Lisa's fear and distrust of other people, along with her absolute sense of vulnerability following the relationship's end, caused her to avoid getting support from friends and family. Although Tom may have acted similarly to Lisa in terms of causing the relationship's demise, he may have been a bit more likely to talk about his pain and get support. Finally, after dealing with depression, Lisa decided that she must remain extra-cautious in future relationships. Also, she identified an internal flaw that might be playing a role in her rejections – her appearance. As such, she decides to make some improvements to her appearance before dating again.

An example of how life experiences impact the Social Protection System is provided in **Figure 1.**

Common Core Beliefs

Although everyone has their own unique self network based on their life experience, you will often find common core beliefs shared by people. Some of the more common core beliefs that psychologists (including myself) tend to see in therapy include:

- "I am inadequate the way I am"
- "I am defective in some way"
- "I am unlikeable"
- "I am unlovable"
- "I am a failure"

There are many others, but they likely overlap with these beliefs to some degree. In fact, these beliefs overlap somewhat as well, and it is not uncommon for someone to have more than one. These beliefs are highly likely to make people feel vulnerable to rejection and social isolation. Therefore, people with these beliefs often have highly sensitive threat appraisal systems.

One of the more interesting things about these beliefs is that people are not always aware of their existence. In fact, you probably have met people in your life who appear to be incredibly confident and self-assured, yet underneath the exterior, they hold some of these beliefs. In my own professional experience, I have worked with many people who would be considered highly successful, popular and seemingly confident. Yet, when you strip away their defence mechanisms, you can see these core beliefs at the heart of their psychological problems. We will explore how defence mechanisms add an extra layer of complexity to people's personalities, and to the Social Protection System, in Chapter 5. However, now it is time to examine another important component of the Social Protection System – our responses to pain.

Figure 1. *The development and impact of core beliefs*

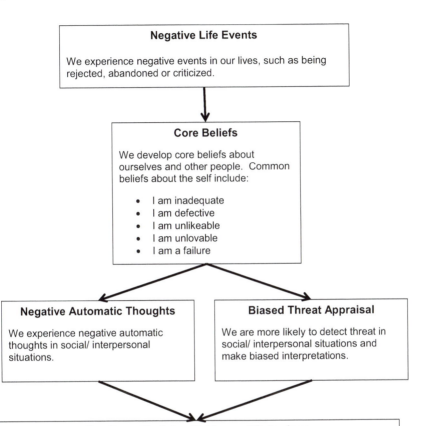

Chapter 4

RESPONDING TO THE PAIN OF REJECTION

Thus far, I've discussed the development of core beliefs and how these beliefs affect the first stage of the Social Protection System – threat appraisal. Once we've appraised an event as being an act of rejection, the physiological response of the body is often outside of our control, especially if the reaction is intense. It is very difficult to control strong physiological arousal. This is one of the reasons why psychologists often recommend to patients with Panic Disorder to not try and change their breathing once a panic attack starts. When someone is feeling mild to moderate anxiety, deep breathing exercises can be helpful. But there is little to be done once the body starts panicking. Similarly, if we believe we have been rejected, and the rejection is significant, there is nothing we can really do to stop the brain from processing this experience as social pain. In other words, the threat appraisal stage essentially determines whether or not the body and brain respond to threat. However, it is important to note that re-appraising a rejection experience (i.e., realize that you were not necessarily rejected) can have the effect of minimizing pain (see Chapter 6).

However, it is not only the pain or anxiety of rejection that causes people significant problems. People's responses to the pain of rejection can often make things worse. Pain and anxiety are uncomfortable – they are supposed to be. These physiological reactions, along with our basic emotions, were designed to motivate us in some way. People often feel depressed or feel pain for a reason – something has happened in their lives that demands attention. It could be broken arm or a broken heart. In either case, some kind of response is often required by the person. However, as with most things in life, some responses are more helpful and adaptive than others.

The next two chapters examine unhealthy or problematic responses to rejection. The focus of the current chapter is on more immediate, short-term reactions, whereas Chapter 5 examines long-term changes due to rejection.

Unhealthy Responses to Rejection

As stated above, I draw a distinction between short and long term reactions to rejection. Long term reactions involve changes in beliefs, behaviour and personality that can be observed over an extended period of time (i.e., months to years). These reactions will be covered in the next chapter, and are best conceptualized as prevention efforts. The person is changing some aspect(s) of themselves to prevent future rejection. The remainder of this chapter is devoted to more immediate reactions to rejection. These reactions typically occur soon after the rejection experience.

There are three broad types of reaction to rejection (reviewed at the end of the chapter in **Table 3**). The first is people's efforts to fight the source of threat – to attack the offending party. The second relates to the person's attempts to control their pain. This primarily involves efforts to get rid of the pain as quickly as possible. Finally, the third type of response is our attempt to gain insight into what happened, in order to determine whether a significant change is required.

Because this book primarily deals with problems associated with the need to be liked, the remainder of this chapter will focus on the dysfunctional elements of these responses. Things like rejection and the need to be liked are normal human experiences. However, normal human needs and reactions can easily become dysfunctional (ex: eating and eating disorders; anxiety and the anxiety disorders).

Pain following rejection can be a normal and healthy reaction. It is unpleasant and hurtful by its very nature. However, it is important not to confuse unpleasant with "unhealthy" or "abnormal." Unfortunately, this seems to be a common mistake, especially in North America, where unpleasant psychological states like pain, rejection, sadness and anxiety are considered pathological. Both the increase in the number of psychological disorders identified by health professionals and the growing sales of the pharmaceutical industry are evidence that our society is moving toward a collective belief – that unpleasant experiences are intolerable and must be avoided. This belief is erroneous and often leads to additional problems.

An old Buddhist expression I once heard while studying mindfulness meditation says "one arrow in the chest is bad, but two is worse." It basically means that when something bad happens, it is best to try and avoid adding to your misery. In the sections that follow, it should become clear how poor reactions to rejection can initiate a vicious cycle, which renders the person in a worse state than they would have been otherwise.

Fighting Back

There is an abundance of research evidence which shows that people often respond to the pain of rejection by getting angry and fighting back[19]. The degree to which someone will feel angry is likely in proportion to the amount of pain felt from the rejection. And the intensity of the pain is determined by the meaning attached to the rejection. If someone feels pushed away, but knows logically that the other person still likes or loves them, then the pain may be minimal. However, if the person believes that the other person is pushing them away because they dislike their key traits and qualities, then the pain will be much worse.

Research on anger, aggression and social pain shows just how harmful this combination of feelings can be[20]. People who feel the pain of rejection often feel angry and will sometimes choose to express this anger in some way. They might engage in passive-aggressive behaviour (ex: making mean jokes; "forgetting" to do important things you ask them to do). They might become very critical and even verbally abusive. The pain of rejection can be so severe and unmanageable that it leads to violence, including sexual assault and murder. Rejection is one of the more common precursors to husbands killing their wives, and feeling rejected by women can increase feelings of anger in men, leading at times to acts of sexual violence.

It is not always clear why rejection leads to these outcomes, although there are a number of potential reasons. First, attacking your attacker might stop any ongoing rejection. For example, if you are an adolescent who feels picked on and excluded at school, an act of violence (ex: punching one of the bullies) might put a stop to some of the poor treatment. Or, if you feared that your spouse was going to leave the relationship, then devaluing her and perhaps even making her fear you might prevent the rejection from occurring.

There is also the catharsis hypothesis – the idea that expressing the anger you feel in response to rejection might help you feel better. However, catharsis has been known by psychologists for a long time to be an ineffective strategy. In fact, letting out all your anger in one big burst can have the opposite effect, and make you feel worse. There may be even more basic and biological reasons for acting aggressively and violently in response to rejection. Revenge is a basic emotion that arises when we feel another person has caused us an injustice. Perhaps attacking another person who has rejected you is just a natural urge that we are wired to feel.

Regardless of the reasons for why rejection leads to aggression and violence, choosing to engage in this kind of behaviour usually only makes things worse. It should be clear why violence and emotional abuse leads to poor outcomes, and are not a good idea for numerous reasons.

However, it is not always obvious how more subtle forms of aggression can negatively affect relationships. In fact, people are not even always aware of when they are acting aggressively in response to rejection. For example, you might find yourself talking behind your friend's back after they forgot to return your phone call. Or, a wife might "lose" sexual interest in her husband in response to his spending more time with his friends. These behaviours can be subtle forms of punishment, directed toward someone who may or may not know that they've hurt the other's feelings. Clinically, I've witnessed such behaviour in my relationships with clients, who might cancel an appointment, arrive late to sessions, or offer a backhanded compliment, all because they felt hurt by something I said or did (unintentionally, of course).

The real problem with these more subtle forms of aggression is that they only serve to make things worse because many of these retaliatory acts are going to cause hurt feelings and defensiveness on the part of the targeted person, who may then respond with their own retaliation, and so on and so forth. Indeed, heated arguments and even break-ups can occur because the hurt feelings from perceived rejection were not appropriately handled. Because subtle forms of rejection are so common and pervasive, there are indeed times when people will not know that they've hurt another person's feelings. If the person does not know why they are being treated poorly, it only gives them reason to act aggressively in turn. Even when someone does know that they've accidentally caused another person pain, it is usually unhelpful to simply attack this person because aggression leads to defensiveness. When someone is defensive, they are not going to be in a position to listen carefully, consider the other person's arguments and concerns, and problem-solve. They are only going to focus on protecting themselves from the attack, which might include attacking back with criticisms of their own.

There are times when it is appropriate to express anger toward a loved one following a hurtful behaviour, however, this decision requires tact and must be reasonable. Simply yelling and throwing things around the house rarely accomplishes much.

Pain Control

Rejection is an unpleasant experience. Rejection can involve pain, negative thoughts and a host of negative emotions (ex: depression; anxiety). As such, people will want to move past the rejection experience as quickly as they can – some more than others. Indeed, the inclination to get rid of unpleasant experiences is fairly normal. Nobody likes to feel depression, anxiety or pain. People generally don't like to be frustrated, angry, bored or disappointed. We also dislike hunger, headaches and heartburn. It is by evolutionary design that we dislike these things. These things are unpleasant for a reason – they motivate us to take some kind of action.

When we are threatened in some way (anxiety), cannot attain a goal (frustration) or have been wronged by another person (anger), the emotions that accompany these experiences exist to grab our attention because we may want/ need to react to these problems. Similarly, pains in the body often indicate that some response or change is needed. The point is that these negative experiences are necessary and important to our lives. Of course, knowing this does not make them less unpleasant.

Unfortunately, some people are better able to handle these unpleasant experiences better than others. Some people feel compelled to get rid of these experiences as quickly as possible, using any method they can. These people engage in what psychologists call **experiential avoidance**. Experiential avoidance refers to a person's persistent attempt to avoid negative thoughts, feelings and/ or physical symptoms. While it is true that no one enjoys feeling the pain of rejection or negative thoughts and feelings, some people are more sensitive than others. Therefore, people who engage in experiential avoidance *really* don't like these negative experiences, and will try to avoid them as much as possible.

For example, if someone does something unethical, they can (1) ponder their actions and process their guilt, or (2) avoid thinking of the mistake and suppress their emotion. In this example, the former strategy can be thought of as an 'acceptance' or 'willingness' to experience negative thoughts and emotions. The second strategy is 'avoidance.' Although avoidance might feel better in the short term, people who use this approach risk having more problems in the long term.

The following are common responses to rejection that can cause more harm than good. People who use experiential avoidance in general, or those who are highly sensitive to rejection specifically (or both), are most likely to use these strategies.

Alcohol/ Drugs/Food

Generally speaking, when it comes to the avoidance of pain and negative emotions, chemical substances that alter the body and brain's current state are a popular choice. It makes sense. If you feel anxious, a glass or two of wine can calm you down. Feeling sad? There are many drugs that can be used to quickly fix this problem – both legal and illicit. Bored late at night or stressed at the end of your day? Eating fast food or sweets can help make you feel better – at least for a little while. One could argue that North Americans have become less and less able to handle unpleasant experiences - that we are so incapable of dealing with life's daily problems, that experiential avoidance is the norm. This would explain the ever-increasing use of prescription medication and overconsumption of fast food.

Rejection experiences and their consequences can lead to substance abuse of all forms. This type of response is probably more common following a relationship break-up. Drinking or taking drugs (including medication) to deal with the pain and negative thoughts (ex: memories) of a lost relationship is not uncommon. I'm sure many readers have witnessed this behaviour first hand, or have even engaged in this type of behaviour themselves.

It is not necessarily the case that taking <u>any</u> chemical substance to cope with negative experiences, including rejection, is wrong or unhealthy. Using one of these substances in a moderate amount can be fine. For example, following a relationship break-up, spending an evening eating a bucket of ice cream with friends, or drinking Scotch while listening to Air Supply, may be a reasonable way to cope with the immediate intense pain (see Chapter 6). However, if the binge eating continues for an extended period of time, or the drinking gets out of hand, then you suddenly have a new problem on your hands. Remember that Buddhist expression from earlier? Well, having a relationship end is bad. Having a relationship end and developing an unhealthy addiction is worse.

Inability to Let Go

Sticking with the break-up theme, another type of avoidance strategy is to stay in a bad relationship. Whenever an important relationship ends, more often than not there will be some pain and feelings of sadness. Eventually with time, this pain goes away. This is the mantra often passed down from people who have had their hearts broken to their unfortunate friends currently experiencing a similar fate. They say "just give it time and you will forget about him/ her." This advice is similar to what's recommended for people trying to quit cigarettes – when you stop smoking it will be incredibly hard, but eventually it gets easier and easier, until one day you are free from addiction. Here's the thing – with both smoking and ex-relationship partners, there is one major hurdle to recovery – it is always easier just to give in. This is why so many smokers start smoking again, and why so many people go back to their ex. The latter group tend to think (on some level) "It's easier to just start dating again than to deal with this pain and discomfort." They rationalize this decision by reviewing all the good qualities about their ex and the old relationship. This is a wonderful example of the defence mechanism **denial** – by ignoring an important piece of information (in this case, all the reasons why the relationship is unhealthy), it makes reuniting an easier choice. Consequently, they return to an unhealthy relationship – sometimes on more than one occasion.

For some people, the pain of being rejected by their partner, or the pain of having that attachment broken, is so feared that they never even dare leave the relationship – even if it is unhealthy and/ or abusive. Similarly, believing that you are unlikeable to others can motivate you to stay in a bad relationship because you believe an abusive relationship is the best you can hope to get. This exemplifies a very negative by-product of hopelessness – the decision to avoid making positive and healthy choices on the assumption they will not work out anyway. When faced with the options of staying with an abusive partner and constantly being rejected by people who would be healthy choices (leaving you lonely and hurt), it is sometimes easier to just stay in the unhealthy relationship.

Some people are so haunted by a particular thought following a break-up, that they are driven back into the doomed relationship. The thought that I am referring to goes something like this – "I will never find someone who loves me that much again" or "I will never find a relationship like that again." This type of thinking turns a temporary situation (break-up) into a long-term feeling of hopelessness. Believing that you will never be as a happy with another person for the rest of your life is a very depressing thought, and it is completely understandable why someone would feel horrible thinking this way. However, it does not mean this thought is correct.

While returning to your ex to avoid the pain of a break-up is one option, quickly jumping into a new relationship is another option (commonly known as *the rebound*). Choosing to quickly start dating someone new following a break-up is particularly likely if your sense of likeability was threatened in some way. For example, if you start to question how attractive you are following a break-up, one way to answer that question is to test it out by seeing if someone new finds you attractive. If you can start dating someone new quickly following a break-up, it can have the benefit of (1) easing the pain of the break-up, and (2) making you feel attractive (or at least likeable in some other way) again. I'm not saying this is healthy decision-making – just highlighting the fact that rebound relationships can help ease the pain of a break-up (if only for a short while).

Clinging

Sometimes a relationship doesn't have to end for someone to try and avoid the pain of rejection. The mere possibility of rejection is sometimes all it takes for some people to feel unsafe. Whenever someone feels highly vulnerable to rejection, they are going to look for possible signs and cues in their partners. When such cues of potential rejection are found, some people become "clingy," meaning they become overly dependent on the other person. For example, after a mild argument with a boyfriend or girlfriend, the rejection-sensitive person might respond by trying to spend a lot of time together, and perhaps acting irritable when their partner tries to leave.

A very common issue among people who are insecure in relationships is the tendency to make excessive use of reassurance seeking. Constantly asking the other person if they are "angry" or "upset" with them, or continually checking to make sure the other person is happy and the relationship is good, are a few examples of reassurance seeking. The person who is constantly seeking reassurance benefits from reductions in anxiety when their partner confirms that things are "OK." However, the long-term risk is that their partner will become irritated by the constant requests for reassurance. In the long run, excessive reassurance seeking typically does more harm than good.

Depression and Suicide

Feeling very sad following a serious relationship break-up is common and normal. Some people even experience a clinical episode of depression. The pain of the break-up can be so strong, it can leave people incapacitated. They lose their appetite, motivation, interest, and energy to do things. Imagining a future without the other person causes more distress and feelings of hopelessness. Generally speaking, depression can be thought of as an emotion that occurs in response to **loss**. Typically, the loss is something that brought pleasure or happiness. So, if we lose our job or a loved one dies, sadness and depression are reactions to this depletion of joy in a person's life. Whenever we lose someone we love, or even worse, when we are rejected and pushed away by someone we love, the loss can be crippling. In extreme cases, people decide that the pain is simply too great – their loss is simply insurmountable. As such, they tragically decide to end their suffering by means of suicide (the ultimate form of pain avoidance).

While suicide can easily be understood as an extreme case of pain avoidance, depression is a bit more difficult to understand. When someone is depressed, what are they avoiding? Well, one of the presumed evolutionary advantages of depression[21] is that it compels the person to stay away from other people, or at the very least, from forming close relationships. When one examines the symptoms of depression, it is clear that the disorder renders the person much less capable of functioning. In particular, it makes socializing much less likely. Symptoms such as low energy, low motivation, little interest or ability to take pleasure in activities, difficulty concentrating, irritability, and low self-esteem, increase the likelihood of depression sufferers staying at home, possibly in bed, and away from interactions with other people. Indeed, this is often what happens when people are depressed – they significantly reduce their time spent interacting with other people. Presumably, this is a way of protecting themselves from further rejection and pain. It is also a way to let the current feeling of pain minimize with time – in an uninterrupted manner. There are other features of the depressed person that indicate the operation of a protective function – namely, rumination and self-criticism.

Initial Response and Prevention

Imagine being faced with the following problem: you have to leave town suddenly for a funeral, but you need to find someone to feed your pets while you are out of town. A potential solution is to ask friends to help out, or you can hire someone to take care of them for a few days. This is a very simple example of problem-solving. In this case, the problem was something that was going to happen in the future, and one option is to take some action now to deal with the situation. Problems such as these are manageable because we usually have some element of control – we can do something to either prevent the problem from occurring, or to minimize the problem's effects. So, what happens when you have little to no control over the problem – such as when problems are in the past?

Following a rejection, people are sometimes motivated to understand what went wrong. Was there something they did to cause disfavour in another person? Is there something about them that is unlikeable? Could they have acted differently, or responded to a certain situation in a different way? Answering these questions is seen as important for at least two reasons. First, understanding things usually makes people feel better – there is a sense of closure and clarity that comes with understanding why something happened. The opposite feelings – confusion and uncertainty – typically leave people feeling anxious and stressed. As such, people

62

will often try and reflect on a past relationship or past relationships, in order to gain understanding of past problems. They may also reflect on who they are as people, to see if there is something fundamentally wrong with them. Finding answers to both of these problems could theoretically be very beneficial. The answers might allow the person to avoid problems in the future. Unfortunately, trying to gain insight to these problems on your own and in a depressed state can also make things worse – particularly when people get caught in a process known as **rumination**.

Generally speaking, rumination can be defined as the tendency to repetitively think about problems, usually those that occurred in the past, although they may be currently ongoing. It may also include the tendency to repetitively think and dwell on personal characteristics and traits. As previously mentioned, this rumination process is often initiated by someone wanting greater understanding - someone who wants answers. However, just because the person is able to initiate rumination does not mean they are able to stop rumination. In fact, rumination tends to be a thinking process that is uncontrollable and intrusive. The person feels trapped by the looping of thoughts, ideas and memories. Research typically finds an association between rumination and psychological problems such as depression and anxiety[22].

When it comes to interpersonal stress, such as rejection, rumination makes intuitive sense. By looking to the past for a better understanding of some problem we might then be able to prevent the same problems from happening again in the future. There is something very pragmatic about this intense search for the truth. Unfortunately, this search can cause more problems than solutions. As previously mentioned, rumination is associated with depression and is known to lower most people's mood. The recurring cycle of negative thoughts lowers mood, which makes it more likely for additional negative thoughts to come to mind. Soon enough, people find themselves uncontrollably dwelling on the past and their current problems. The presumed path to insight and answers ends up being more like a racetrack – you go round and round and always end up in the same place.

Another consequence of rumination is that it can lead to significant re-interpretations of the past that may or may not reflect reality. Following the loss of a relationship or some kind of rejection you may start to re-examine memories from the past. For example, you might view a fight with an ex-partner differently after ruminating about it. What was once a mild disagreement over dinner 6 months ago is now considered to be evidence that people dismiss your opinions and treat you poorly. Or, the failure of the relationship itself might be viewed as evidence of your own inadequacy – a negative thought that never occurred prior to the ruminative thinking.

Rumination can be about events that took place years ago. However, people can and do ruminate on things that occurred just minutes ago. For example, after briefly chatting with a friend you just met on the street, you may replay that meeting over and over in your head. You might ruminate on little things that were said, or minute behavioural details, to get a sense of whether the other person likes or is happy with you:

- "Why did he pause after agreeing to have coffee next week?"
- "Maybe I shouldn't have told that story?"
- "Man, she really didn't find me funny at all."

This experience of ruminating on events can completely change our perception. Thinking repeatedly of an event can have the effect of changing our memory of it. If rumination is used with frequency, the danger is that we are left with many more negative memories of awkward social experiences than is actually the case. For example, individuals with social anxiety tend to remember bad social encounters more than good ones, particularly after ruminating about these negative encounters[23]. This solidifies their negative core beliefs. If you believe on some level that you are unlovable or defective in some way, then ruminating on every negative social encounter (real or negatively interpreted) will only add confirmation of the original belief. In this way, people can get caught in a prison of negative beliefs and biased perception.

Self-criticism is another thought process that gets used by people who have been rejected or are depressed. Similar to rumination, this is a strategy that on the surface seems as though it could serve a useful function. By examining our flaws in detail, we might identify those that interfere with being liked and accepted by others. However, there are at least two potential problems with this approach.

First, people do not always have the flaws they perceive, or at the very least, are exaggerating the severity of the problem. For example, women sometimes believe their weight is a problem following a relationship break-up. Men might believe they are sexually inadequate. These might be actual problems, or they might not. Unfortunately, people can sometimes identify problems when there are none, and use either little to no evidence to support their thinking.

The second problem with self-critical thinking is that it is often not used effectively to deal with actual problems. The process *should* look something like this:

1. You identify a problem that is based on evidence. For example, you think "I can be rude and inconsiderate." This is based on several people's comments and past incidences.

2. You think of how you can change, and then take action to make the necessary changes.

Unfortunately, people make mistakes with either step, or even both. For instance, you might identify a problem that does not actually exist. Then, you either fail to fix it, or you try and fix the problem (which doesn't exist) using a faulty strategy. For example, Ryan believed that he was emotionally weak and incapable of handling life's problems. There was little evidence to support this type of thinking – in fact, his ability to cope was about average when compared to other people. However, rather than fix this perceived problem, Ryan beat himself up over this shortcoming every time he became emotional under stress. The one change he did make was to never ask for help or support when stressed or sad – in order to prove to himself and others that he was not weak. In this example, the whole process is filled with errors and mistakes – all in the name of self-improvement.

As mentioned, self-criticism can be irrational if the person identifies a flaw that does not exist. For example, if someone rates their physical attractiveness to be very low (ex: 3/ 10), when in fact there is plenty of evidence to the contrary (ex: compliments; history of dating), it is clear that a flaw is being created through negative thinking and biased perception. Alternatively, people's self-evaluations might be relatively accurate, but their personal standards are too high. Sticking with the same example, I have worked with many young adult women who rate their physical attractiveness as being a 6 or 7/ 10. This is technically above average (5/ 10) and should be considered a positive trait. However, their accurate self-assessment actually makes them depressed because they want to be a 9 or 10/ 10.

This shows that in order for self-criticism to be effective, you must not only be accurate in your self-evaluation, but also make sure that the standard you are evaluating yourself against is realistic and healthy. Otherwise, simply ruminating on your flaws will leave you feeling needlessly depressed.

Overall, rumination and self-criticism are not always destructive processes, but when they are done *alone* and in a *negative mood state*, the whole process could quickly take a turn for the worse. My advice is this – if you seriously want answers to important questions, it is usually a good idea to have objective input. Finding someone, whether it be a trusted friend or a health professional, to help your search for answers is probably the best approach (see Chapter 6).

Table 3. *Responses typically seen in response to the pain of rejection.*

Types of Responses	Examples
Fighting Back	<ul><li>Physical Violence</li><li>Passive-aggressiveness (ex: aggressive humour; "forgetting" to do important things)</li><li>Emotional abuse (ex: degrading the other person)</li><li>Criticism</li></ul>
Pain Control	<ul><li>Use alcohol, drugs and/ or food</li><li>Remain in unhealthy relationships</li><li>Cling (ex: excessive reassurance seeking)</li><li>Depression/ Suicide</li></ul>
Initial Response and Prevention	<ul><li>Rumination</li><li>Self-criticism</li></ul>

Chapter 5

PREPARING FOR FUTURE REJECTION

Up to this point in the book, we have covered the various ways that the need to be liked can 'go wrong'. From negatively biased threat appraisal, and dysfunctional core beliefs to unhealthy decision-making and excessive self-criticism, the need to be liked can cause emotional problems, such as depression, anxiety, substance abuse and overeating (to name a few). The current chapter addresses the final, and perhaps most important, stage in the Social Protection System. After experiencing the pain of rejection, **how do we use what we've learned to better deal with relationships and rejections in the future?**

We are all wired to avoid pain. This means that we are going to act in ways that increase the likelihood of safety. When I am working with a client whose life has been significantly affected by the pain and fear of rejection, I inevitably ask myself the following question – what does this person do to keep safe and avoid pain? The answer to this question varies from person to person, as there are many ways of keeping safe. In this chapter, I will outline the more common strategies used by people to protect themselves from social pain. I hope it becomes apparent to readers that these safety strategies are very much engrained in people's personality, and affects them in very fundamental ways (i.e., their thinking and behaviour).

We can categorize these various safety strategies according to the fight, flight and freeze responses outlined earlier in the book[24]. Doing so not only helps organize these strategies, but also highlights how basic biological responses underlie more complex psychological responses. We are wired to respond to threats using one of these three approaches. Thus, it should come as little surprise that humans' long-term safety responses are similarly organized around these same biological imperatives. In fact, the immediate response strategies described in Chapter 4 similarly resemble these response options.

First, I must clarify the term "threat?" One type of threat is rejection itself (including its associated pain). However, there is also a second threat – one that is significantly linked with the need to be liked. Whether a person is **likeable** or not (i.e., their 'likeability') is a critically important factor because it is a significant predictor of rejection.

Earlier in the book, I discussed the formation and influence of core beliefs. Although there are many core beliefs of the self, I believe that the likeability core belief is among the most important, and that many other beliefs are simply smaller parts in the overall evaluation of likeability. Many of the other beliefs relate to the question "Am I likeable to other people?" Beliefs such as "I am defective?," "I am a failure?," and "I am stupid?" are lower-level components of the likeability core belief. You can think of the relationship between these other beliefs and the likeability belief as being similar to an argument. If you want to argue a point, you present premises, which support the conclusion. These other beliefs are like premises – they will influence the final conclusion. Hence, these beliefs are very important because they help us answer the likeability question. For example, if you think you are a failure, unintelligent and unattractive, then the answer to the likeability question may be "No, I am not likeable to other people." If you believe that you are not likeable, then a fundamental need is not being met and this has consequences.

Recall that fundamental needs serve a purpose – they help us survive (evolutionarily speaking). If a need is not being met, there's a problem. When someone believes that they are not likeable to other people, this will be viewed as a threat. Even though we live in a world where we technically do not 'need' other people, we are designed for a world where we do. As such, the brain will respond to the threat of unlikeability. In the same way that we tend to seek safety from the pain of rejection, people also want to avoid the threat of being an unlikeable person.

To say that someone fights, flees, or freezes in response to an immediate physical threat is to be literal – they fight, run or remain petrified. To use these terms when discussing rejection and the belief of unlikeability is more metaphorical. However, as will become apparent in the personality descriptions below, the use of these terms is quite appropriate. Therefore, the remainder of this chapter is organized into these three descriptive categories.

Fight Response

When faced with the possibility of being physically attacked, one option is to fight the threat. Well, when faced with the possibility of being rejected by another person (ex: spouse), one option is to do whatever it takes to make sure that this feared event fails to materialize. How do you prevent rejection from occurring? One option is to be more likeable. While this might seem like a reasonable strategy, the problem is potentially twofold: (1) people can go too far in their pursuit of being likeable, and (2) they can maintain this strategy for too long a period of time. In other words, they can **overcompensate.**

Overcompensation
The psychological process of overcompensation basically involves two steps. The first step is the identification of a defect or flaw. The defect is often a perceived deficiency in one of the following traits:

- Intelligence

- Social skills (ex: sense of humour)
- Physical attractiveness
- Particular abilities (ex: athleticism)
- Social Status (ex: high SES)
- Career success

Notice that each of these qualities is valued by people around the world. The value and importance of each trait will vary from person to person and from culture to culture. For example, some people will value success in their career as more important and critical to their likeability than social skills, and vice versa. What we value depends on our developmental experiences and immediate cultural surroundings.

In general, someone with many of these qualities is more likely to be liked by others than someone lacking in such valued characteristics. It is not surprising when someone who is attractive and smart has more friends than someone who is lacking in these traits. However, this will not always be the case (ex: if you were unattractive yet very nice and friendly, you might have more friends than your attractive counterpart who is considered cold and distant), and the issue is indeed more complex than this, but I am trying to use a simplified approach in order to explain a more general process.

Each of the above noted traits exists on a continuum, and everyone can be 'rated' on each trait (ex: a 5/10 on attractiveness; 8/10 on sense of humour). As such, you could theoretically compute a total "Likeability" score for each person by summing the ratings for each trait. This would give a general idea of how likeable someone is to other people. The general point is that people with higher likeability scores would find themselves being liked and in more relationships than those who have lower scores.

Some readers might wonder why certain traits are not included in the list above. For example, being a nice and empathic person should affect how acceptable and likeable you are as a person. This is absolutely true. Nice people are liked better than mean people. However, being nice is usually not a quality that people worry about in terms of overall personality. In fact, I don't think I have ever seen a client in therapy overcompensate for not being nice enough. This may reflect the fact that *being a nice person* is generally under one's full control, whereas the other qualities are not entirely under people's control. You might say that being nice is something anyone can do – but not everyone can be attractive or smart. Thus, from an economics standpoint, the latter traits are going to retain more currency. Consequently, people tend to be more focused on these more valued traits. Now, when I say "valued," I do not mean more important. Let me elaborate a bit further.

When it comes to liking another person, knowing whether the other person is nice and warm is often very important. Even if someone has most of the above-mentioned traits, if they treat others poorly, it seriously lowers the probability of being liked. Therefore, being "nice" is an important quality. Interestingly, despite being important in terms of its impact on being liked, people do not always *value this trait in themselves*. They are more interested and concerned with having the above-mentioned traits. This leads me to comment on one of the more interesting aspects of being a clinical psychologist. If there is one thing I have learned in my years of work as a psychologist, it is this – **people often use a different set of standards to evaluate other people than they use to evaluate themselves**. Specifically, when I ask clients to tell me which qualities are most important in other people, they invariably list the following qualities:

- Honesty
- Loyalty

- Empathy
- Trustworthiness
- Warmth

Therefore, if someone lacks these qualities, they are generally considered unlikeable by the client. Conversely, when I ask these same clients which qualities about themselves make them unlikeable to others, they usually list the traits mentioned earlier (ex: "I'm not smart enough" or "I'm not attractive enough"). Notice the pattern? Other people are liked for being nice, while clients feel their probability of being liked is dependent upon more superficial qualities. Thus, when discussing the process of overcompensation, we are really dealing with these more superficial traits.

Returning to the task of defining overcompensation, the process of identifying flaws is one that can be done alone, or it can be facilitated by other people. For example, being repeatedly criticized by another person (ex: a parent criticizing their child's poor school performance; being mocked and socially isolated by peers in high school) can contribute to the identification of personal flaws. In order for the flaw to evoke a response in someone, it typically has to be considered a valuable social asset. For example, if you believe you are a poor driver, this likely has little effect on your self-concept. However, if you believe that you lack athleticism, and you attend a high school where that trait is highly valued, it might be seen as an important flaw.

Once a flaw is identified, the person often feels compelled to act. This leads to the second step in the overcompensation process – the person tries to increase the value of one or more of the other traits in order to improve his or her level of likeability. Earlier, I discussed the idea of being able to calculate a likeability score by summing ratings across the various traits. Well, imagine that someone's score is 35 (this number is fairly arbitrary and is only used to make a point). Now imagine that the person in question believes that this likeability score is too low. It is too low because a certain trait is deficient in some way. There's a flaw. Well, there are two ways to increase the likeability score at this point. The person can (1) try to directly improve the flaw in some way, or (2) they can increase their rating on another trait(s). Simply put, the persistent attempt to cover up and hide flaws is called overcompensation. What exactly does the term 'persistent attempt' refer to?

The term 'persistent attempt' refers to the amount of time and effort used to hide the deficiency or flaw. Let me offer an example to explain this point and to describe the various routes to overcompensation. If Allison believes she is unattractive, and she believes that attractiveness is highly important to being likeable to other people, then she can overcompensate in two ways. First, she can take excessive measures to correct the perceived defect. This might involve surgery (ex: plastic surgery) or excessive dieting if the concern is with weight (alternatively, if this were an example of a man, he might try to 'bulk up'). Allison might also spend a significant amount of time assessing her appearance and searching for flaws. She might spend a lot of time and money buying clothes and make-up. She might also exercise frequently. Clearly, Allison is devoting a significant proportion of her time to hiding or changing the perceived defect. I am not referring to more minor and common strategies. Simply shopping, using make-up and exercising do not mean someone is overcompensating. However, if the person is engaging in these behaviours more than the average person, and is doing so in the belief that change in appearance is absolutely necessary to be liked and accepted by others, then this is overcompensation.

Alternatively, Allison might try to hide one defect by increasing the value of another trait. She might focus all of her attention on another trait to overcompensate for the flaw of being unattractive (or at the very least "not attractive enough"). For example, she could work incredibly hard at school in order to be seen as very smart and accomplished. Or, she might try and sharpen some aspect of her social skills, such as sense of humour. By making people laugh, she is able to find an alternative route to being liked and accepted.

In extreme examples of overcompensation, Allison might overcompensate by making personal changes in multiple domains. For example, she might focus excessively on her appearance, while simultaneously attempting to be seen as highly intellectual, athletic and funny. Again, it is not the mere attempt to have these qualities that is dysfunctional – but when someone feels compelled to spend considerable time and effort focusing on these things, all in the name of hiding flaws and being liked, this should be considered maladaptive overcompensation.

However, I hesitate to use the word *maladaptive* because there are times when overcompensation is quite necessary and understandable. For example, if as a child you were made to feel as though you were a failure and unlikeable (ex: teachers and parents' critical comments; bullied and/or rejected by peers), you might cope with this stressful period by focusing on an area of strength. You might study hard and become the top student in your class. Or you might try to gain attention by being the class clown and making your peers laugh. By making such 'self-improvements' and earning praise along the way, you are able to cope with this difficult period. It makes sense for people to overcompensate in order to cope with periods of life stress. However, under these circumstances, the problem often lies with letting go of such overcompensation.

As mentioned earlier, there are at least two problems with overcompensation. The first problem dealt with going too far in terms of hiding defects and trying to be more perfect. The second problem with overcompensation occurs when it is used to cope with a stressful period in one's life, but the person then fails to let go of this strategy.

To further describe how this might look in real life, I will provide a clinical case example, which is fictional in nature:

Ted is a 35 year-old junior executive at major accounting firm. He has built an excellent reputation in the company through years of hard work. He was hired by the company after receiving his MBA from a top university where he excelled and won the respect of his peers and faculty members. He is also well-liked outside of work by close friends and family. Some people consider him to be too confident at times, and he will occasionally seem arrogant. He works out at the gym 5 times per week, and buys a lot of nice clothes. He is quite concerned with his appearance, and spends a fair amount of time trying to maintain a certain image. He is single and dates frequently. He can never seem to find the right woman, which leaves him feeling lonely. But he enjoys the attention he gets by being single, successful and in great shape.

Although Ted appears confident, there are aspects to his personality that indicate some insecurity. For example, he can get quite anxious in social situations, particularly public speaking. Also, he really struggles with critical feedback and craves special attention (ex: he gets bothered when others receive praise at work; he often searches for other people's flaws).

When Ted was in high school, he was occasionally mocked for his appearance. At that time, he was short and very thin. He also got beaten up by another student in front of many of his peers, which he found humiliating. He never dated in high school and would rarely even speak to girls. He was completely self-conscious and shy most of the time.

In this example, Ted is overcompensating. He developed some negative self-beliefs in high school, such as "I am unattractive" and "I am unacceptable the way I am." He turned his attention to academic performance and eventually to his career. He also worked on his appearance, which has paid dividends in terms of attention from the opposite sex. Many people would empathize with Ted. He went through a very difficult period – a brutally awkward phase of development. In turn, he felt compelled to correct his flaws and become highly successful. This change in behaviour has served him quite well. The problem is that he has gone too far in the other direction, and is refusing to let go of the overcompensating behaviour. His attempt to be the perfect male is interfering with his ability to form close connections to women and stay in a committed relationship. Also, his high-maintenance appearance and job leave him little time to enjoy other aspects of life (ex: spending more time with family and friends). Ted's discomfort with showing flaws makes it difficult to be himself around others – he feels he has to always *act* a certain way to win approval.

Perhaps the most damaging aspect of his overcompensation is his failure to be a regular person. Regular people have flaws and defects, which make them more likeable und understandable to others. Whenever people meet someone who seems perfect, it can make them feel uncomfortable. At worst, it prevents close connections from forming. No one is perfect and we can all take comfort in knowing that we all have flaws. We can relate to each other's experiences by knowing the good and the bad. It is impossible to relate to someone who acts as though they are flawless – because no one knows what that experience is like. When we meet people who have similar flaws to our own, the common ground that is shared makes us feel closer to that person. In Ted's case, no one can honestly relate to him.

Not only does Ted's overcompensation interfere with others getting to know him, but it also prevents a genuine self-understanding from occurring. Ted has become so focused on creating a shell – the external appearance of perfection and likeability – that he has lost a connection with himself. Over time, he has lost the ability to discern the genuine from the disguised aspects of himself. On the surface he is a very confident, successful and attractive person. Underneath, there remain the insecurities that were present in high school. Why is this? Doesn't overcompensation get rid of these beliefs? No, it does not.

Overcompensation allows someone to hide the flaws – to use smoke and mirrors to fool others that you are not who you appear to be. And it can often come with praise and reinforcement. But all the praise and reinforcement does not hide the fact that the *perceived* flaw is still there. And it is still present – otherwise, people who overcompensate wouldn't feel compelled to do so. They would drop the overcompensation and move on with life. The fact that Ted continues to behave as though he were hiding something only confirms that this is indeed the case. So, how does someone change these core beliefs that underlie overcompensation? I will address this issue in the final chapter.

Earlier, I wrote that people do not often overcompensate for a perceived lack of qualities like friendliness and niceness. However, that does not mean that these qualities cannot be used as *overcompensating behaviour*. In fact, people who believe they are flawed and very susceptible to rejection can become overly nice and self-sacrificing in order to win approval from others. When I use the term self-sacrificing[25], I am referring to the tendency to consistently put the needs of others ahead of your own. These individuals are often seen as being overly passive, and can be taken advantage of by others. They have difficulty being assertive because they fear angering other people and being rejected. Typically, the self-sacrificing person learned at some point in life that being overly ingratiating to others lead to benefits (ex: compliments; friends), and that it certainly helped prevent negative evaluation, criticism, and rejection by others. Indeed, it is difficult to hurt another person's feelings when they are often so nice.

One of the problems with self-sacrificing behaviour is that it can have negative consequences in relationships. When people are constantly doing things for other people and persistently refusing help when needed, it can make people feel uncomfortable. Self-sacrificing behaviour creates tension in relationships by virtue of there being an imbalance in reciprocity. Imagine that you meet a friend for lunch every week, and every time the bill comes your friend says "I'll pay for it." Eventually, you might feel uncomfortable never contributing to the meals. You would probably assert your position at some point and say "No, you're not paying! I'm getting this one." The reason for this discomfort is that people often seek balance in relationships – which is why reciprocity in behaviour is fairly common. When someone holds the door for you, you may feel compelled to then hold the next door for them. This is normal and healthy. However, when people don't allow us to reciprocate – when they never accept help (ex: never talk about their own problems, but are eager help with yours) - it creates tension. The receiver of these benefits feels uncomfortable and possibly even guilty about the state of affairs. This is not good for the relationship.

It is often the case that self-sacrificing individuals are overcompensating for some perceived defect, or are so afraid of the pain of rejection, that they are willing to subvert their own needs for those of others. Similar to the other forms of overcompensation discussed earlier (ex: striving for intellect, success, attractiveness, etc.), self-sacrificing can push others away and prevent close connections from developing.

The common theme among people who overcompensate is that they do not always feel comfortable revealing personal flaws. This does not mean they will try to hide all flaws – as long as it is a *safe flaw*. A **safe flaw** is one that matters little to the person (ex: driving ability; ability to cook). Another possible safe way of discussing a flaw is through self-derogatory humour. By making fun of oneself about a particular flaw (ex: being overweight), the person is able to diffuse the emotion inherent in the flaw and what it means. While such style of humour is usually harmless on its own, when used in conjunction with other overcompensating behaviours and when used consistently to avoid discussing painful self-aspects, it is considered dysfunctional and unhealthy.

I hope it is a little clearer why overcompensation is similar to fighting as a protection response. The common denominator is the decision (perhaps unconsciously) not to be passive about the threat – to meet the threat head on. In the case of overcompensation, the intention is to kill the threat of rejection and the belief of unlikeability by changing who we are in some important way. By constantly striving to hide flaws, we actively fight against our fears of rejection and unlikeability. However, overcompensation is not the only method of fighting, although it is probably the most common.

Excessive Criticism

Another 'fighting' strategy is excessive criticism of other people. When people feel vulnerable to social pain or believe they are unlikeable, they can fight back by trying to identify flaws in other people. This approach is like attacking your predators before they have a chance to attack you. As they say, "the best defense is a good offense". The criticism can be either overt or covert. Overt criticism occurs when you communicate the criticisms to another person (i.e., "behind his/her back"), or to the target themselves. Covert criticism occurs when you search and identify flaws, but keep the judgments to yourself.

People who are excessively critical may search the specific flaws that are most concerning to themselves. For example, if you are someone who has doubts about your level of attractiveness, then you may be more likely to criticize others' appearance. Criticizing other people in this way helps to minimize the pain of dealing with the perceived flaws in yourself.

To understand ourselves, we often need information from other people. For example, I can only know that I am funny if people laugh at my jokes. How do I know if I am attractive? Well, I can observe others' behaviour towards me (ex: flirting) to help answer this question. One of the ways by which we learn about ourselves is through social comparisons. Social comparisons are attempts to understand where we stand on a certain trait relative to another person. For example, if you notice that Tony always gets As on his exam, Claire always gets Cs, and you always get Bs, then you have an idea of how intelligent you are relative to these people. Similarly, you can compare yourself to other people on many dimensions in order to get an understanding of the type of person you are. This process can help shape your self-image and self-esteem.

So, what happens when we see another person who is more attractive or smarter than us? Well, this type of social comparison can make us feel sad or threatened in some way, especially if attractiveness (or intelligence) is very important us. What happens when we notice many people who are more attractive? This seems to happen with more frequency in North America, as people (especially women) are confronted with media images of others who are exceptionally attractive – often in a fake way (ex: airbrushing in magazines). This can negatively affect people's self-image – it can be depressing to constantly feel below average on an important trait. This is where criticism can come into play.

By criticizing other people for their flaws, it helps reduce the discrepancy between you and other people. This helps explain the immense popularity of gossip magazines and websites – by knowing that celebrities have flaws, it helps make us feel less defective in some way. There are two possible routes to lowering the discrepancy between ourselves and other people. First, we can criticize others on the trait we feel most insecure about. For example, if you worry about your weight, then constantly recognizing and criticizing other people who have weight problems can help reduce the discrepancy, and minimize the pain of our own flaw. Second, by criticizing the other person on other qualities, you can reduce the discrepancy between yours and their overall likeability. Sticking with the gossip magazine example, criticizing Angelina Jolie for something other than her appearance can make oneself feel better ("Sure, she's pretty, but I bet she's really dumb") – or at least, not feel as inadequate, if physical attractiveness is a source of personal concern.

It is important to know that these two fight responses, overcompensation and criticism of others, are not mutually exclusive. People can, and often do, use both approaches on a regular basis. In fact, each of the responses discussed here and below (flight and freeze) can be used at various times by the same person. It is often not the case that someone uses one approach, and one alone. Metaphorically speaking, people will sometimes choose to fight and sometimes choose to flee. However, one response option may dominate, meaning the person will use one strategy more than others.

Flight (aka Avoidance)

When someone feels they are at risk of, or are actually being physically attacked, they can try to run away. The flight response can be just as effective as the fight response – assuming you can outrun your attacker! When it comes to protecting the self from rejection and unlikeability, the person always has the option of simply avoiding the negative aspects of these threats. There are a number of ways in which people can avoid social pain and the negative emotions associated with believing one is unlikeable. You can avoid thoughts, relationships, emotions, social events, etc. Basically, there are all kinds of things that can be avoided – all in the name of keeping oneself safe.

Let's start with relationships, as they are a very common target of avoidance. The rationale behind this type of avoidance is very simple and straightforward. If you're not in a relationship you cannot get hurt by rejection. While the logic is simple, the actual manifestation of avoidance in relationships is more complex, as there are various forms of avoidance behaviour. Specifically, avoidance behaviour can range from obvious to subtle. As such, people may not always be aware that they are engaging in avoidance at all.

The simplest form of avoidance is to exclude people from your life. This is an extreme example of avoidance, but it does occur for some people. I have had a few clients who are so sensitive to rejection that they place a strict limitation on who they allow in their life. While I have never worked with anyone who excluded all people from their life, there are cases where the exclusion only allows for 1-2 close relationships.

It is important to make a distinction between two types of social avoidance. First, there is avoidance of interactions with people, generally speaking. This is common among people who are shy or socially anxious, and feel very uncomfortable doing things like meeting new people, striking up conversations with strangers, or doing anything that could be evaluated (ex: public speaking; dancing; singing). The primary fear for these socially anxious people is potential negative evaluation from other people – the fear that other people will judge or criticize them in some way. Being negatively evaluated by other people is similar to rejection, in that the person's behaviour is creating a distance between the two of you, as they identify a flaw that makes you less acceptable to them (or others). Another way to think of negative evaluation is that it is evidence of unlikeability. We don't have to see a bear to fear that one is nearby. We might hear something or see other evidence that we're in danger. Similarly, rejection does not have to occur outright – as evidence of unlikeability can create fear all the same (i.e., it indicates that rejection may be near).

The second form of social avoidance is that of close interpersonal relationships. Sometimes the fear of negative evaluation and the fear of close relationships are related, but this is not always the case. Someone could be very outgoing and socially uninhibited – talking to strangers and being the life of the party. But this same person might avoid close relationships (either friendships or romantic relationships, or both). The fear here is that getting close to someone will only lead to rejection and pain. Oftentimes, the person predicts that once someone gets to know who they really are as a person – once others see their flaws – they will leave. Such beliefs of abandonment often have their origins in early life rejection. For example, if a child was always made to feel abandoned by his or her parent(s), or if an adolescent was socially alienated by his or her peers, this could create a belief of unlikeability, sensitivity to rejection, and the tendency to over-predict abandonment.

It is important to note that simply because someone avoids getting close to other people, does not mean that they necessarily avoid relationships. A common pattern found among people who use the avoidance strategy is that they often have a lot of "acquaintances," but not many close friends. They socialize with people at work, have lunch with colleagues from time to time, play in local sports leagues, and belong to organizations and clubs. These particular individuals can have many social interactions on a daily basis, but there is a lack of close bonding in each instance. The person does not feel comfortable getting close to anyone in particular, and therefore is able to maintain a sense of comfort and safety.

To complicate matters even further, it is even possible for someone to have a long-term romantic relationship with another person and avoid emotional intimacy. Being in a long-term relationship with another person does not necessarily mean that either person feels particularly connected to the other. Indeed, people can be married for decades and feel no more connected to their spouse than to anyone else. In this type of situation, the person is able to avoid developing a deeper connection with their partner in various ways:

- Avoid discussing emotions
- Avoid affection
- Keep conversations at a relatively superficial level
- When the other person needs support or help, only provide problem-solving, not empathy and emotional support

Similar to overcompensation, there are occasions when interpersonal avoidance is necessary. Think of a child or adolescent who is relentlessly bullied by peers or abused by a parent. It only makes sense that they protect themselves from this pain – so, avoiding relationships and people can serve a very useful function. But as with overcompensation, a problem arises when the person continues to hold onto this strategy when it is no longer necessary. Thus, there are times during my own therapy sessions when I am forced to say to clients – "I understand that you had to protect yourself at age 13 because of that awful environment. But that environment has changed and the threat is gone. It's time to start letting go of the defences." However, the difficulty with having clients let go of these defences is that they have worked so well to this point. The person believes that they have been able to avoid a significant amount of pain by keeping this avoidance strategy. It can be difficult for them to foresee living without their defences – they would feel too vulnerable.

However, another problem that arises in therapy while trying to encourage someone to drop their defences is that they sometimes have lost opportunities to develop certain skills. For example, if Sally started using avoidance strategies at an early age, she may lose out on the acquisition of skills that come naturally with development and social interactions (i.e., social skills). Similarly, if she avoided close romantic relationships, she may not know how to give emotional support to another person, or how to discuss not only her own emotions, but those of other people as well. These kinds of situations make dropping one's defences more difficult, but it is certainly possible if done correctly.

While avoidance of close relationships and people represent one form of avoidance behaviour, the person can also choose to avoid the painful emotions associated with rejection and the belief of unlikeability. This is often accomplished by changing the way the person physiologically responds to stress, pain and negative emotions. Eating food, drinking alcohol, abusing drugs (including prescription medication), and even self-harm (ex: cutting the skin) are all strategies that can help someone avoid negative emotions and social pain. These efforts to numb or decrease feeling, generally speaking, are often reactionary strategies, meaning they are typically used in response to negative experiences. However, they can also be used habitually, as a way of living life. One of the obvious drawbacks to using these strategies is that they often create whole new sets of problems.

Freeze (aka Passive Acceptance)

When a person or organism is facing an immediate physical threat, they can respond simply by freezing. It is always possible that the predator in this situation will have mercy and back off, but in most situations this is the least effective protective response. It appears as though the person or organism is simply giving up in this situation. Similarly, when people use freeze strategies in their daily life, they are passively giving into the social pain that they see as inevitable, and to the belief of being unlikeable that they are certain is true. In fact, the person lives their life "as if....[insert negative belief] were true." For example, the person using this approach may live life as if....:

- ...they were a failure, and would fail at most things they try.
- ...they are unlikeable, and would likely be ignored or rejected by new people.
- ...they are unacceptable to others, and would be abandoned eventually in most close relationships.

I could add as many "as ifs...." as there are negative self-beliefs. The thoughts that are most important in this context are related to unlikeability and predictions about being rejected. Whenever someone buys into and accepts these predictions, their lives have little hope for long-term happiness. As such, people who have identified and then passively accepted their flaws, tend to feel hopeless about the future.

Whenever someone believes they are a failure, they tend to avoid efforts to become successful in a particular domain. For example, a salesman at a company may avoid asking for a promotion because he assumes that his request would be denied, or that he would simply fail at the higher level position anyway. There are shared aspects between avoidance and passive acceptance strategies. In this case, there is avoidance of potential rejection by having his request for promotion denied.

The distinguishing feature between *avoiding* and *freezing* tends to be the level of hopelessness. The person who avoids believes that they might be OK in the long-run as long as they can avoid the threat at hand. The person who freezes believes that the threat is inevitable, and there is little that can be done to change things. In the present example, it is considered avoidance if the salesman believes that he could do an excellent job with a promotion, but the potential for rejection (i.e., being turned down for the promotion) is too risky. Conversely, he is using passive acceptance when he avoids asking for a promotion out of the presumption that he would never succeed at the next level anyway.

Using a more interpersonal example, imagine two fictional people (ex: "Sally" and "Greg") - one uses avoidance and other uses passive-acceptance strategies. Sally avoids relationships in order to prevent rejection. Greg avoids relationships because he simply assumes that all relationships are going to eventually fail anyway. The difference is that Sally believes the relationship could work, but it is too risky, while Greg passively accepts the belief that he will never find someone to love. In the end, they both avoid getting close to other people.

It can be very confusing for people who are dating or married to someone with a passive-acceptance response style. At times, the relationship can be going well and both of them seem to be quite happy. Then, one spouse or partner will suddenly withdraw from the other person and become more distant. This occurs because the "freezing" partner allowed themselves to briefly feel comfortable in the relationship before realizing (remembering) that they should not get their hopes up – the other person will probably reject them eventually, or the relationship will simply not work out ("they never do"). This kind of approach-avoidance behaviour can occur for many people with the passive acceptance response style. They always seem to remind themselves that nothing will work out positively, or that they are inherently flawed and unlikeable, and so why bother trying?

The passive acceptance response style can be dangerous at times, particularly when the person believes they are deserving of abuse and feels little urgency to leave the abuser. They remain in the relationship and go through life tolerating the abuse. They act as if they are deserving of this abuse – as if this is the kind of life befitting someone who is of little value to others. Leaving the relationship is useless because they are unacceptable to others, and so there is little chance of getting into a genuinely healthy relationship anyway. The passivity and hopelessness in these kinds of situations are often bred early in life – being raised in a dysfunctional environment that engrains a sense of hopelessness and self-loathing.

In fact, people who use the freeze response often feel more comfortable in an unhealthy relationship than a healthy one. Living life for such a long period of time as if one is unlikeable and defective, in addition to chronically being mistreated by others, can make the positive elements in life difficult to bear. For example, when you accept the fact that you are inherently unlikeable to others, it is very difficult to take a compliment. Furthermore, it can be downright unbearable to exist in a relationship where the other person treats you with love and respect. These kinds of experiences are too foreign and unfamiliar. The person is more willing to believe negative feedback because it is more consistent with their worldview. Remember, these people live life as if... most things were negative. So, when something positive comes into their lives, in whatever form that might be (ex: compliment; success; some period or happiness), the automatic reaction is to assume it is an error, an aberration that is to be disbelieved.

It is common for people with this response style to constantly degrade and mock themselves. Feelings of worthlessness and depression are also common with this group. In a way, these types of behaviours do offer some element of protection from rejection. By putting yourself down first, you could be beating someone to the punch. It's easier to avoid failure and rejection if you never try to succeed. Also, when you are feeling low and depressed, people are less likely to treat you poorly. In this light, you are more likely to be seen as a wounded animal who poses little threat to anyone else. In fact, this type of self-degrading behaviour might even elicit sympathy from others. However, notwithstanding these potential "benefits" from the freezing response, this is an approach that is probably least effective in terms of coping with life, avoiding rejection, and avoiding the pain and negative emotions that come with negative beliefs. There is always an element of masochism to this response style, which leaves the person continually dealing with some degree of pain.

Concluding Comments

As mentioned earlier, the response styles (for review, see **Table 4**) outlined in this chapter are not mutually exclusive. At times, there are overlapping features between styles (ex: between avoidance and passive acceptance). Furthermore, while most people tend to use one response style more than another, it is typically the case that people use more than one approach. So, someone might use overcompensation, but occasionally use avoidance in relationships. It is the numerous possible combinations of these response styles that adds flavour and diversity to people's personalities.

Understanding how these safety response styles operate explains why two people can have identical backgrounds, and yet appear so completely different[26]. For example, imagine two fictional people – Kim and Karen. Both were sexually abused as children, and consequently developed beliefs about being worthless and unlikeable. Kim learned to cope by overcompensating – she became a very successful lawyer who devotes much of her life to her job. Karen learned to cope through avoidance and passive acceptance – she is addicted to prescription medication, abuses alcohol, and drifts from one unhealthy/ abusive relationship to another. Both women might appear very different on the surface, but their history and motivation is quite similar

One final point to be made, and one that is very important, is that people are not always aware of (1) the response styles themselves, and (2) why they are using the response style. When it comes to ideas surrounding the unconscious mind, people might be sceptical and question whether there is an unconscious. After all, isn't this an old Freudian theory? Well, although previous theories of the unconscious mind were not always accurate, there is overwhelming research evidence supporting the existence of the unconscious[27]. To say that something is unconscious is to some degree accurate, but also a bit misleading. The brain can and does process information and make decisions without us being explicitly aware of it. A simple example of this is driving a car over a long distance. It seems that a person can think of just about everything except driving during a long road trip. Meanwhile, the brain unconsciously scans the road and controls the motor functions of the body. The fact that we have significant memory gaps for parts of trips like these supports the notion that there was unconscious processing (i.e., there will be no memory for things that we did not pay attention to).

A slightly more complex example of unconscious processing comes via research on subliminal messages. The brain can detect and understand brief pieces of information presented for durations as short as 17 milliseconds![28] When scientists flash words on a computer screen at this speed, people report that they see nothing, but there is evidence that the brain saw it. There is plenty more research supporting the existence of the unconscious, and a full review is outside the scope of this book. Needless to say, the fact that the brain can manipulate information and control our decision-making without our explicit knowledge is fascinating and sometimes difficult for people to accept.

When it comes to decisions about how best to protect oneself emotionally, this decision-making process can be partly conscious and partly unconscious – and anywhere in between these ends of the consciousness continuum. Awareness of things like threat appraisal and core beliefs will differ from person to person. Sometimes people are aware of why they decide to avoid something like a social event, and sometimes people just decline an invitation and think "I just don't feel like going," – which is to say that they may not be fully aware of why they've made this decision. Similarly, I've had clients who know quite well what their core beliefs are, while others have come close to knowing (i.e., they have a feeling that something is wrong with them, but don't quite know how to articulate this exactly), and others who have no idea whatsoever. Think of the character presented earlier in this chapter – Ted. He probably has no idea about many of the psychological processes which operate daily for him. Indeed, this is one of the main reasons people seek the services of a psychologist – when you cannot see or understand something yourself, it can be useful to have an expert help identify them for you.

When thinking about the response styles presented in this chapter, it is important to remember that most people are probably not completely aware of why they do these things. These response styles operate like defence mechanisms. A psychological defence mechanism is any attempt by the mind to protect itself from uncomfortable perceptions, thoughts, emotions and memories. Being unable to remember aspects of a traumatic experience (a symptom of Post-Traumatic Stress Disorder) is an example of a defence mechanism. The brain is trying to defend itself from feeling the intense negative emotions associated with a horrible event. This is understandable. It is also understandable why the brain would do other things to protect itself as well – like overcompensating to prevent rejection and avoiding painful thoughts regarding one's flaws and defects. It is important for clients in psychotherapy to know that their brain can act on their behalf without them knowing. Hopefully, this knowledge helps prevent them from engaging in self-criticism over past actions associated with the response styles discussed in this chapter. It is unfair and pointless to blame oneself for an unconscious decision made at age 11.

Table 4. *Long-term response styles of people who have been significantly affected by the pain of rejection.*

Type of Response Style	Examples/ Descriptions
Fight	• **Overcompensation** ▪ Hiding or masking a perceived defect or flaw in some excessive manner ▪ Ex: Becoming a very successful businessman to hide insecurities concerning lack of social skills • **Excessive Criticism** ▪ Constantly trying to identify flaws in others in order to manage the negative feelings associated with your own flaws.
Flight	• Avoid thoughts and emotions associated with rejection and/ or unlikeability • Avoid social interactions • Avoid developing close connections with people
Freeze	• Based on previous rejection experiences, you presume that rejection is inevitable in life, and so you live "as if" rejection will ultimately occur.

Chapter 6

FIXING PROBLEMS WITH THE SOCIAL PROTECTION SYSTEM

After having introduced and reviewed the Social Protection System, and how this system can cause psychological problems, it is now time to review strategies that can be used to manage problems at each stage. This chapter is organized into two parts. First, I will introduce the basic components of Cognitive Behavioural Therapy (CBT), which is arguably the most popular and empirically supported psychological treatment available today[29]. Second, I will demonstrate how to use these CBT strategies to manage problems that arise within the Social Protection System. It is important to note that this chapter is not a substitute for professional treatment. The ideas presented here are most likely going to be helpful from a psycho-educational standpoint. In other words, while the strategies presented here will be sufficient for some people, those with more serious issues are likely going to require the services of a registered psychologist. However, for this latter group, the present chapter may be useful in terms of becoming familiar with coping strategies in order to make changes in their life. However, when psychological problems are serious, it is often the case that professional help is required.

CBT Basics

As mentioned, the coping strategies presented here are based on concepts originating from CBT. The basic foundation of CBT can be understood by the following three principles:

95

1. Negative emotions and even serious psychological problems are caused by dysfunctional thoughts, beliefs and behaviours,

2. The thoughts, beliefs and behaviours of people can be changed in order to treat these problems, and

3. There are a number of strategies that can be used to make these changes.

Therefore, when addressing a psychological problem, it is very important to know how cognition (ex: thoughts, beliefs, perceptions) and behaviours are contributing to the cause of the problem. Next, we must figure out how to change these cognitions and behaviours.

The Role of Cognition

Have you ever heard the following expression:

- 10% of stress is what happens to you, and 90% of stress is how you respond

I usually don't like quotes, clichés, and expressions like these because they are often overvalued as being useful for handling stress and life problems. However, I like this quote because it approximates my own professional view of psychological problems. Let's start with the first part of the quote – 10% of stress is what happens to you. This refers to the fact that negative things will happen in life. When they happen, you can expect to feel some degree of stress or other negative emotion. This is normal. Negative emotions are normal. It is normal to feel depressed, anxious, angry, guilty, shameful, etc. at least some of the time. As such, I often advise clients against efforts to immediately get rid of negative emotions when they come into their lives. As mentioned earlier in the book, emotions serve a purpose - they give us information. So, whenever you feel stressed or are experiencing a negative emotion, the first step is to recognize what emotion you are feeling and figure out why it is there.

Now, many people might think that first piece of advice is pretty straightforward – it's easy to know which emotion you're feeling. This is often true, but sometimes it does require additional effort to sit back and think about what you are feeling. Some people have a difficult time recognizing exactly what emotion they are feeling. Others don't even take the time to figure out what they're feeling. For example, you might be out for a walk and notice a co-worker walking on the other side of the street. You think you see your co-worker look at you, but then keep walking without saying "Hi." Many people in this situation would have an emotional reaction. But what is the emotion here? Embarrassment? Anger? Sadness? Disappointment? Before you can fix a problem, it is best to get a clear understanding of it. When it comes to fixing problematic emotions, you must first figure out which emotion(s) you are dealing with.

Once you've figured out the emotion(s) you are feeling, you must then ask – what is causing the emotion? Or, why am I feeling so stressed? This is where things can get tricky. This is also a good time to return to the quote from earlier. A proportion of our emotional reactions will come from negative events, and another proportion will come from our *interpretation of these events*. Let me use a concrete example to explain this further.

Imagine that two women are going through a divorce – Elaine and Mary. Both were married for 10 years and have children. Both women feel stressed, sad and anxious following the divorce. However, Mary is having a more difficult time than Elaine. Mary often feels more depressed than Elaine and her depression is worsening. Also, Mary and Elaine are having different thoughts about their divorce. Elaine thinks "This is awful, but I'll eventually move on." Mary thinks "I'll never find another person who loves me."

First, it is completely normal for both women to feel stressed, sad and anxious. Whenever someone has an important relationship end, it is very difficult. Second, I hope that readers are able to recognize why Mary is more depressed than Elaine. Thinking and believing that she would never find another person to love her is worsening her depression. The connection between this thought and her emotional reaction makes complete sense. Imagine if you really, honestly believed that from this day forward, you would never enter into a romantic relationship where the other person loved you. It is a very depressing thought – one that is not uncommon in these situations.

Let's examine Mary's situation a bit further by returning to our earlier questions – what is the emotion and what is causing it? Well, there are a few emotions, but the main one is depression. It is being caused by two things: (1) the loss of an important relationship, and (2) the belief that no one will ever love her again. So, we have a fairly accurate assessment of the problem. Now what?

Many negative emotional reactions will have these two causal factors – a negative event and an associated interpretation. When it comes to coping with stress and negative emotions, it is absolutely critical that these factors be examined for validity. This means we should ask ourselves a few questions:

1. Am I sure I perceived the event accurately?
2. Are my thoughts about this event valid?

Let's start with the first question. In this case, the answer is pretty easy. Mary is indeed getting a divorce. She is losing an important relationship. However, people do not always correctly interpret the meaning of life events. A constant theme throughout parts of this book has been that social situations are often ambiguous. This can make it difficult to correctly evaluate and understand life events. Did I just get rejected? Did that person seem upset with me? Did I make a mistake? These are questions that people are sometimes left asking themselves after a social interaction. So, how do you assess the accuracy of something that is ambiguous? You look for evidence and alternative possibilities.

Let's return to the example used earlier. You walk down the street and a co-worker doesn't say "Hi." Is this person upset with you, or does he/she not like you? You have to think of the evidence and alternative possibilities. First, let's examine the evidence. Whenever you consider evidence, you have to use facts. In this case, there are certain facts you will want to consider. Did you get into an argument recently? How has this person treated you in the past? Do you have a good, solid relationship with this person? If your relationship with this person has been fine, and you cannot think of a reason why they would avoid you, then you have no good reason to believe they think negatively of you.

Next, you have to consider alternative explanations for their behaviour. Did they notice you? Sometimes people can look in your direction, but not notice you. Maybe they have a lot of on their mind and weren't paying good attention to their surroundings. Maybe they did notice you, but did not feel like talking because they are feeling sad or stressed. Maybe they are shy and avoided making contact with you. There are numerous possibilities.

The rule of thumb is – if you have no good evidence to think something negative has happened, then assume things are fine. Whenever people assume the worst in social situations, regardless of the evidence, they are making the "safe choice" (see Chapter 3), but not necessarily the most realistic or adaptive. The goal should be to make the realistic interpretation. Otherwise, you create more stress and problems for yourself. This is a very important point – people often create their own stress when they make negative interpretations of ambiguous or innocuous social situations.

In terms of the second question ("Are my thoughts about this event valid?"), it is again critically important to examine your thinking honestly. People often make what psychologists call cognitive errors. **Cognitive errors** are negative thoughts that are based on poor logic and little evidence. Psychologists have identified a number of cognitive errors that people tend to make, with the 10 most common being[30]:

1. **MIND READING**

    Mindreading occurs when you assume that another person is thinking negatively about you and there is no logical reason to make such an assumption. For example, you are having coffee with a friend and arbitrarily assume her silence means she is upset with you (ex: "She is thinking something negative about me").

2. **CATASTROPHIZING**

    Catastrophizing occurs when you make negative predictions (i.e., catastrophic predictions) about the future without much evidence for these predictions (ex: "If I go to this party, people will see that I look uncomfortable and awkward and they will not want to hang out with me again. I will never make any friends.")

3. **ALL-OR-NOTHING THINKING**

    All-or-nothing thinking occurs when you evaluate situations, events, or relationships as being "either-or." You see things as often being black-or-white, with no shades of grey. For example, when Ted leaves a party and thinks he hasn't made a large, positive impression with people, he tells himself "That was a complete failure of a time." For Ted, you are either admired or unimportant – there is no in-between.

4. **EMOTIONAL REASONING**

    Emotional reasoning occurs when you believe something to be true because it "feels" that way. You might know logically that you have not been rejected, but it *feels* like you were rejected – therefore, you assume you have been. For example, Maria knows that her friends did not invite her to go to the

100

museum because she hates museums. But she *feels rejected* and this plays the largest role in her emotional reaction of sadness.

5.   LABELING

Labeling occurs when you label yourself as being a certain *kind of person*. It usually occurs after something bad happens. For example, after making a small gaffe on a date, Ian calls himself an "idiot." People sometimes do this in a humorous manner, which is typically fine. However, if you notice that you often beat yourself up over things, and it is really out of proportion to the mistake, then it is a thinking habit that should change.

6.   MENTAL FILTER

Whenever you receive positive and negative information, if you only focus on the negative information, it is called mental filtering. For example, Greg's girlfriend recently told him that although his jokes can be a bit aggressive, he is overall a very funny guy, and that she loves his sense of humour. Afterwards, Greg is only able to think about the mild criticism he received.

7.   OVERGENERALIZATION

Overgeneralization occurs when a negative event happens and you assume that more bad things are going to happen. You perceive the negative event as the start of a pattern. For example, after two unsuccessful relationships, Lisa believes that all future relationships are pointless, and she ends up feeling hopeless.

8.   PERSONALIZATION

Personalization occurs when you take responsibility for negative events, even though you are not at fault. In other words, you take a negative event and assume you are the cause of it. For example, Bob's wife has been feeling stressed and depressed recently because her mother died and she has been struggling to adjust to a new job. However, Bob feels guilty because he thinks "I should be doing more for her during this tough period."

9.   SHOULD STATEMENTS

Whenever you think that things should or must be a certain way, it is considered **should** thinking, which is similar to perfectionism. For example, Shelly hates her appearance because her nose is slightly too big for her liking. She thinks "In order for me to be considered attractive, all features of my face should be relatively flawless." This is obviously faulty thinking.

10. MINIMIZING OR DISQUALIFYING THE POSITIVE

Whenever you ignore the positive things that happen to you, it is called minimizing or disqualifying the positive. For example, imagine that for most of your life you make friends easily and get positive feedback from others about qualities that are likeable. Then, a co-worker admits to not liking you as a person. If you start believing you are unlikeable, then you are clearly disqualifying a large proportion of information that says you are likeable.

Although these cognitive errors are relatively common, each of these types of thoughts has problems with logic and can lead to a range of emotions, most notably anxiety and depression. These kinds of thoughts are negatively biased. In ambiguous situations, it may not be clear whether something positive, neutral or negative has transpired. Whenever your default choice is negative, you are not seeing reality – your thinking is biased. It is important for people to recognize when they are making these cognitive errors. Returning to the coworker example, you might have several thoughts, each of which could represent a cognitive error. For example, you might think:

- "He/she thinks I'm annoying" (mindreading)
- "I must have done something wrong" (personalization)
- "I know I've been rejected because it feels like I've been rejected" (emotional reasoning)
- "He/she will probably ignore me at work" (catastrophizing)
- "I wonder if other people at work will start to ignore me as well" (overgeneralization)

These kinds of cognitive errors are also known as **automatic thoughts**. They are called automatic thoughts because they can occur very quickly in response to situations. Indeed, people can have these thoughts and not even recognize their presence. The thought quickly occurs at some level of consciousness, and the person feels the subsequent emotion. It is for this reason that awareness of these thoughts – catching them when they occur – is so very important. If you do not take time to identify the cause (cognitive error) of a problem (stress/negative emotion), you are unlikely to find a solution.

The Role of Behaviour

In addition to biased thinking, it is important to examine one's behaviour. Behaviour has significant effects on our thinking, beliefs and emotions. Whenever people act a certain way, it has the potential to affect their perception of things, including their perception of themselves (known in psychology as *self-perception theory*). For example, if you often go to parties and socialize with people, you are likely to think of yourself as being at least somewhat outgoing and sociable. If you tend to choose abusive partners and remain in unhealthy relationships, you might think of yourself as worthless.

Think of it this way. If you had a close friend who was in an abusive relationship, and you encouraged that friend to remain a victim of abuse and to abuse drugs, the friend would probably think poorly of you. They would think "Hey, this so-called friend of mine doesn't care about me at all." Well, if you replace the friend in this example with yourself – when you decide to remain in an abusive relationship and abuse drugs – you reach a similar conclusion (consciously or unconsciously) – "Hey, I don't care about me at all." At the end of the day, you will evaluate yourself in part by the things you do. It is hard to feel good about yourself if you are doing negative things, and it is hard to feel bad about yourself when you are doing positive things. Thus, beliefs we form about ourselves are affected by our behaviour.

Behaviour can solidify or maintain negative beliefs as well. Imagine you believe that getting close to others only leads to disappointment and hurt feelings. The rule is – avoid getting close to people to avoid getting hurt. Following this rule will only serve to maintain the original belief because you never get the opportunity to put your

103

belief to the test. Beliefs only change when you are exposed to experiences that prove the belief wrong. Unfortunately, when someone avoids relationships, they never get an opportunity to change the underlying belief.

Behaviour also affects other psychological factors, such as motivation, energy, emotions and automatic thoughts. People are more likely to feel additional motivation once they start doing an activity. In this way, behaviour can oftentimes precede motivation. Many people assume that motivation must come first, and then you do something. However, it can be the reverse as well. For example, you might not want to study for an exam, but once you spend 5 minutes doing so, it gets easier to continue studying (once the ball gets rolling…). The behaviour was needed to increase motivation.

Engaging in enjoyable activities can also improve energy and positive emotions, which is why it is often recommended at the start of treatment for depression. Remember, emotions happen for a reason. Some people assume that happiness is a trait or default emotion, meaning it should be present most of the time. But happiness is not a trait, it's an emotion. And unless there's a reason to feel happy, why would that emotion be present? Some people believe that happiness comes by having possessions – "I have a big house, two nice cars and a well-paying job, so I should feel happy right?" Having material wealth doesn't lead to happiness, it creates a different feeling – security. If you want to feel happy then you typically have to do something positive or pleasurable – have a coffee with a friend, watch a movie, go swimming, etc. The point is that we can use behaviour to directly influence and control our emotions, energy levels, motivation and thinking. Engaging in activities that are pleasurable is one of the simplest ways of changing negative emotions.

Returning to the example from earlier involving Elaine and Mary, both women could improve their mood by doing something they enjoy – something that often made them happy in the past. It could be spending time with friends and family or taking a day at the spa. This won't "cure" their depression, but it can help ease the pain.

CBT and the Social Protection System

The remainder of this chapter focuses on how to use CBT strategies to manage the problems inherent in the various stages of the Social Protection System. Only those stages that are under our direct control are covered, namely Threat Appraisal, Response to Pain, and Planning for the Future.

Threat Appraisal

Threat appraisal is a very important stage, and serves an important function. It allows people to recognize threats of rejection and unlikeability when those threats are indeed present. Have you ever met someone who just didn't seem to have very good social skills? They were not reading other people's cues and feedback correctly, either because they didn't care or they lacked the skill set to do so. Such people run the risk of social exclusion if they don't improve their ability to detect problems in social encounters, relationships and aspects of themselves.

When there is sufficient evidence to believe that someone is upset with you, doesn't like you, or no longer wants to have a relationship with you, it is important to be aware of this information. It is important to know because you might be able to rectify the problem. You could decide to make changes in the relationship, or make changes to yourself. The latter change could be important for maintaining relationships with others (ex: realizing that you are too defensive and sensitive with others, which makes it less likely that others would want to interact with you).

Given that detection of rejection is necessary and important, it is not helpful to recommend that all rejection threats be ignored because it helps avoid the pain of rejection. However, it is also important to ensure that you do not swing to the other end of the continuum – appraising everything as a threat to keep yourself safe from rejection. The goal should be to try and make as realistic an appraisal as possible. Realistic appraisals offer a nice balance between seeing threat when it is present and knowing when it is safe to be social and interpersonal with other people.

It is very difficult, and in some cases near impossible, for some people to stop the detection of possible rejection. Their brains are just so good at finding threat. The good news is that you don't have to stop detecting threat because there's a second component to threat appraisal – interpretation. So, while you might detect potential rejection in many social and interpersonal situations, you can always manage the social pain and other negative emotions by taking the time to examine your interpretations. Having a bias is not a problem if you are able to correct it.

Unfortunately, making a correct interpretation of a social situation is made more complicated by ambiguity. It is not always clear in interpersonal encounters what other people are feeling, thinking and doing. As such, while trying to make the most realistic and appropriate interpretations in social and interpersonal situations, please bear the following points in mind.

First, people have their own motivations and goals in interpersonal interactions. Therefore, not everything can be taken at face value – not even indications that the other person doesn't like you. For example, when someone seems disinterested or aloof around you, it might be because they like you. They might be acting aloof in order to appear cool, or to avoid making themselves vulnerable in some way. People have all kinds of interesting beliefs when it comes to impression management. They might think "It's important never to seem too interested in the other person when you like them." Or, they might think "By showing someone that I don't really care about them, it will make them try harder to get my attention." These are not necessarily useful ways of thinking, but the take home point is this – people have their own ideas and agendas when it comes to interpersonal interactions and relationships, and it often has nothing to do with you.

Second, and similar to the first point, you should always consider the possibility that other people's psychological issues make them act in ways that have nothing to do with you. If someone seems to act rude or rejecting, they could actually be feeling shy, anxious, depressed, frustrated, angry, etc. It is important not to immediately attribute their actions to something you have done. For example, if your friend has not been returning your calls lately, it could be true that he/she is upset with you, but it might also be true that they are pre-occupied with something else in their life. Personalizing problems by assuming that you are the cause of others' behaviour is not helpful.

Third, be mindful of how your own behaviour affects other people. The clients I see in therapy will often describe to me stories about how other people ignored them at a party or other social event. And they say something like – "It was not a biased interpretation, no one talked to me!" In these circumstances, the client is right in that other people tended to avoid them. But when I ask the client what their behaviour was like at the party, they often report staying quiet, avoiding eye contact and generally keeping to themselves. Now, the client knows why they acted this way – they were shy and did not want to risk rejection. However, other people do not necessarily know this. One of the unfortunate and cruel ironies of social interaction is this – when people are acting shy, they sometimes appear cold, distant and unfriendly. People are not choosing to avoid interaction because they don't like you – they are not interacting with you because they're worried you will reject them too.

Finally, beware of emotional reasoning! Let's say that you've re-appraised an encounter with someone and determine that you were, in fact, not rejected. Unfortunately, although you may have changed your thinking, you might still have a "feeling" or "sense" that you've been rejected, or that you are unlikeable or unacceptable. This is quite common for many people. It is as if they have two voices in their head – one is telling them that everything is fine (based on logic), and another that is always trying to make sure they never feel completely comfortable or happy.

It is not uncommon for my clients to say "I know I have friends and family who love me, but I *feel* like I am defective and unloveable." This usually happens with people who have longstanding negative core beliefs. When you have felt a certain way about yourself for a long time (ex: "I'm a loser"), it can be hard to get rid of this feeling or belief. During therapy, it can be as if clients kill the negative, low-self-esteem part of themselves, only to have the "ghost" of this former self come back to haunt them – to try and convince them one last time that they are unlikeable.

My advice is to recognize this feeling for what it is – an old false alarm part of the brain that is always trying to scare or depress you. The fact is, whenever reality and evidence tell you one thing, and a feeling or intuition tells you another, always go with the evidence. If you keep reminding yourself of the evidence against these negative feelings, they will occur less frequently over time.

In the end, accurately evaluating the meaning of social interactions and others' behaviours can be very difficult. There will likely be incorrect interpretations made at times, even if you use CBT strategies. However, by using these strategies you can at least keep these mistaken interpretations to a minimum, and take comfort in the fact that you are using healthy thinking and decision-making. Over time, the ability to identify errors in thinking and make corrections gets easier with practice. Automatic thoughts won't completely disappear, but your ability to handle these biased thoughts will improve. Such improvements can make real differences in a person's relationships and their mental health.

Responding to Pain

If you recall from Chapter 4, there are basically three categories of responding typically seen with people who have been rejected – fighting back, avoiding the pain, and trying to heal through various thinking exercises, like rumination and self-critical thinking. Each category has problems associated with it, which can make problems worse for the rejected person. There is overlap among these categories, as they each represent problematic responses. Rather than review each category separately, I am going to offer suggestions and advice for how to handle the pain of rejection in two different contexts: rejection that occurs with people you are close with (ex: spouse; close friends) and those you do not know well (strangers; acquaintances). Thus, my goal with this section of the chapter is to offer healthy response options following rejection, which hopefully will help those people who struggle with the problems that arise at this stage.

There are at least three goals you want to accomplish following a rejection:

1. Manage social pain and negative emotions in a way that prevents the occurrence of unhealthy behaviour,
2. Try and understand the reasons for the rejection, and
3. Problem-solve how best to move forward.

Rejection Involving People We Are Close With

The pain caused by people we are close with has the greatest potential to make life miserable and difficult. The feeling that comes with being pushed away, excluded, and even abandoned by the people we care about can be incredibly stressful and painful. But regardless of how terrible an act of rejection feels, people can take comfort in knowing that the pain will decrease with time. Sometimes, the pain requires no significant response, and it simply diminishes on its own. In other cases, the person has to be proactive in their recovery. Regardless, I am firm believer that although other people have the potential to cause us pain, we can play a significant role in determining whether that pain is maintained for prolonged periods of time.

For some people, the pain of a rejection might never *completely* disappear. You might be someone who has been divorced for 20 years and now remarried, yet feel a little sad after hearing a song on the radio that reminds you of the former relationship. Lost relationships can leave scars, but that's OK. Emotional scars are not all negative – they're reminders not only of the fact that we endured something difficult, but that we're stronger because of these experiences.

The strategies and ideas that are presented here do not have to be employed following every act of rejection. There are times when we might feel a little bit hurt by someone's actions, but on a scale from 1 (no pain) to 10 (excruciating pain), this experience is a 2 or 3 out of 10. In these cases, assuming the rejection does not reflect a deeper, more complicated problem in the relationship, the pain will simply decrease on its own and everyone moves on. For example, imagine that you made a small mistake and said something inappropriate to your spouse, causing them to be upset with you. Your partner might act in ways that are a bit punishing, like not talking or avoiding touch. This is like a mild act of rejection. With time (and some apologizing), things will probably return to normal. Mild to moderate forms of rejection like this one are a part of everyday living. Sometimes people push us away, if only for relatively brief periods of time. Although it may hurt a bit, that is OK. The pain from these smaller acts of rejection will often subside with time and minor effort.

However, when it comes to more serious and painful rejections, it is probably best to be more proactive to help manage the pain and its associated problems. Notice that

110

I used the word *manage* and not *control*. When it comes to psychological experiences like thoughts, physiological arousal, and emotions, people usually do not have complete control over these things, especially if they are intense in nature. But you should not see control as being an all-or-nothing thing. Sometimes we can exert *some control* over a problem. Trying to control things that you cannot will often lead to more problems. For example, trying to control thoughts and emotions (ex: suppressing them) usually only makes them more potent.

Conversely, when you **manage** something you are recognizing what it is that you can control, and then problem-solving how best to take action. Thus, when you get rejected there is nothing magical that can be done to quickly get rid of the pain and negative emotions. You can use alcohol, drugs, and prescription medication, but this doesn't fix everything. These substances numb pain, but that's about it. They won't help you fix the problems in your life, and they won't change your core beliefs. They also won't help you grow and become stronger following a stressful experience. Let me elaborate on this latter point a bit further because it is important.

Whenever we deal with stressful situations, the experience has the potential to make us weaker or stronger relative to the state we were in prior to the stress. If you cannot manage a stressful situation well, and leave the experience feeling less capable and less in control of your life, then you have been weakened by the experience. Conversely, if you are able to manage the stress, and leave the experience feeling more capable of coping with life's problems, you will be a stronger person. These latter experiences can leave you feeling more confident and well-equipped to handle what life throws at you.

In terms of describing the effects of stress on people, I have always enjoyed the analogy of muscles[31]. In order to build muscle, you must put some kind of stress on it (ex: exercising), and then let the muscle(s) heal. With each repetition of stressing the muscle and letting it heal, the muscle becomes stronger. What happens if you stress a muscle too much and don't give it time to heal between workouts? You end up harming your body. And what happens if you rarely work your muscles? Atrophy. You get weaker with time. Thus, stressing your muscles and allowing yourself some rest in between can have long-term benefits. This doesn't mean that working out is always pleasant or fun. Working your muscles during exercise can be painful and unpleasant – but rewarding nevertheless. Similarly, life stress and the rejections we face along the way are unpleasant and painful – but can be rewarding in the long run, in terms of making us stronger psychologically and emotionally.

Now, let's return to the discussion of explicit strategies for dealing with painful rejection experiences. The first thing that I think all people should do is make sure they have understood the situation correctly. This includes re-examining what happened to make sure that they've been rejected. Have you considered alternative interpretations and all of the facts – not the just the negative ones? Also, is there something about you that caused the rejection? Recall that in Chapter 2 I made a distinction between objective rejection and subjective rejection. Objective rejections do not necessarily cause pain, but subjective rejection does because it is so personal in nature. Indeed, there are times when rejection will have nothing to do with us, and so it is important to remind yourself of that fact and accept that it is just a part of life. Let me use an example to explain.

Relationship break-ups do not always occur when there's a problem with one of the people in the relationship. Sometimes, someone will leave their partner because there are problems with the relationship (ex: poor compatibility; poor timing). Or, if someone doesn't want to go on a date, or spend time hanging out as friends, it is possible that their decision reflects things other than you. It is very easy for people who are sensitive to rejection to attribute all rejections to personal causes – those that indicate a flaw in themselves. This may be true, but it should not be assumed until you have good reason to do so. Otherwise, you end up feeling hurt a lot of the time when there is no reason to feel this way. Remember, pain is only useful if it allows us to correctly identify an actual problem. If you consider many things to be rejection, and they are not, it's like needlessly inflicting pain on yourself.

If you're in a relationship and you don't know why your partner has rejected you, it is often best to have a conversation about your concerns. Such conversations work best if you go into the situation wanting to know if there's a problem with you or your behaviour, and with an open mind. If you go into the conversation with a defensive and angry demeanour, there is little chance that things will get resolved. Similarly, if a close friend has been acting in a way that you believe is rejecting in nature, then raising the concern with them can be useful. Inquiring if there is a problem with you or the relationship can be helpful. With anyone we are close with, if we constantly ask whether there is a problem, as a way to feel reassured, this can cause more problems with the relationship because excessive reassurance seeking can have the effect of pushing others away. As such, it is best to only raise concerns when there is good and clear evidence of a potential problem, and not simply because there is a little bit of uncertainty.

Now, starting a conversation with someone in order to try and learn whether there's a flaw or problem with you and how you act is not always easy. But what are the alternatives when you are unsure of why you're being rejected? Ignore the problem? Get angry at the person? Eat bad food or drink alcohol? If someone you are close with is acting in a rejecting manner, it is usually better to try and collaborate to fix the problem. Now, this is not a book on social communication, so how you navigate such conversations is up to you. However, I will offer a few tips:

1.   Always use a calm voice. If you use a tone that is attacking, you will only provoke the other person to enter into a defensive mode, which shuts down

open communication. You make it more difficult for someone to get angry at you or defensive if you talk calmly and at a slow and patient pace.

2. Never assign blame, only highlight how you feel. Rather than say "You always treat me poorly," try saying "I can't help but feel rejected when you don't return my calls." People cannot argue with how you feel, but they will get defensive if you blame them for something.

3. Be concrete when discussing behaviour. Don't use abstract phrases like "You treat me poorly." Tell the person exactly what they're doing, so that they have a better idea of what is happening. So, instead of saying "You treat me poorly," try saying "I feel like I get overly criticized when you're stressed." Talking about things in a concrete way really helps problem solving because you have a very specific problem to work on.

4. Always go into such conversations with a goal – to problem-solve. We're talking about people you are close with, who have indicated that there's something wrong with you or your relationship. Your goal should not be to win an argument – it should be to fix a problem.

5. When discussing personal problems or flaws, you may have competing motivations – protect your ego vs. protect the relationship. Accepting blame and admitting flaws are difficult tasks, but are done for a worthy cause. To make relationships work, you sometimes have to check your ego at the door.

When it comes to discussing personal flaws that are leading to rejection from a loved one, it is important to remember that you do not have to always concede to the wishes of others. People will sometimes reject you in ways that are unreasonable. For example, if you have a trait or quality that most people like, and that you are proud of, should you change because one person doesn't like it? This is where things get more complex, and must be handled on a case-by-case basis.

You might choose to modify your behaviour in some way to accommodate somebody, or you might not change at all, and force the other person to learn to accept or at least tolerate the qualities they don't like. Indeed, tolerating minor flaws in your partner or friends is simply a normal part of being in relationships. Whenever you bring two people together to have a relationship, there will undoubtedly be traits and behaviours in one person that annoy the other. However, it is best not to highlight every minor flaw in the other person. You have to pick and choose your battles.

To this point, we've discussed two of the three goals mentioned earlier – trying to understand the problem and attempting to problem-solve (if necessary). Before moving on to the third goal (learning how to manage the pain of a rejection), I am compelled to quickly resolve what might seem a discrepancy between information provided in Chapters 3 and 6. Recall that in Chapter 3, I wrote about the harmful effects of trying to understand and gain insight following a rejection experience. Specifically, such attempts to better understand rejection, relationships and yourself can lead to problematic rumination and unproductive self-criticism. Some readers might now be confused that I am now recommending they try and find answers.

The goal of gaining insight and better self-understanding is acceptable and understandable, which is why I am recommending it as an option in this chapter. However, the specific process(es) that people use to accomplish this goal is key. Trying to analyze and process multiple pieces of information (ex: thoughts and memories about yourself and relationships) while alone and in a negative mood has much potential to produce bad outcomes.

Therefore, the process of gaining insight should be carried out while placing a premium on objectivity. Using facts and evidence, as opposed to opinions and feelings, is very important. Also, it is often very important that someone else be included in the process in order to maximize the processing of objective information. Although the information gathered through friends and family will not always be purely objective, it is usually a better option than acting alone. Obviously, your choice of people will determine the quality of feedback you receive, so try and choose a level-headed person.

Also, try writing out your thoughts in order to better organize them. The brain is like a computer in the sense that there is only so much processing capacity available for processing information. When we are stressed, anxious and depressed, this reduces the amount of "processing capacity" available for decision-making. Trying to organize your thoughts in such emotional states can be very difficult, so being able to read them can help with thought clarity and organization. Furthermore, depressed mood and other emotions have much potential for biasing your thoughts in an emotional and unrealistic direction. This is another reason for writing out thoughts and relying on objective feedback from others.

Finally, although the goal of gaining insight is important, it is not the ultimate goal in the grand scheme of things. The ultimate goal is to make a decision and act on this decision. Some people believe that insight alone is sufficient for change. As such, they end up trying to think their way out of the problem. This usually leads to **paralysis by analysis**, meaning you spend all your time just analyzing and re-analyzing the same information repeatedly without ever making any changes. Ultimately, you must make a decision (ex: I should change some aspect of my behaviour) and take action.

Now, let's return to the third goal of managing rejection – namely, managing the actual pain that is present following an act of rejection. As mentioned in Chapter 4, there are many ways to handle negative emotions and social pain – eating, drinking alcohol, jumping into rebound relationships, getting angry and seeking revenge, clinging to the rejecting person to reestablish a feeling of safety – to name a few. And as you know, these strategies can often bring more harm than good. My recommendation for dealing with the hurt of moderate to severe social pain is to make use of multiple coping strategies. Although it sometimes only takes one coping strategy to help overcome a difficult problem, I am a firm believer in "the more the merrier" approach to coping. A multidimensional coping response is usually better than a one-trick pony, so to speak. As such, I believe there are a number of coping strategies that are best used in combination.

First, talk to someone about the way you feel. As I highlighted in Chapter 2, research shows that getting social support from another person deactivates the regions in the brain that are causing the pain. Simply talk about how you feel in an honest and open way with other people. It is obviously better to do this with someone you know and trust, including a psychologist if you are working with one. Talking with others about how we feel not only diffuses and soothes strong emotions, it also allows for an opportunity to get an objective perspective. The other person might help you reappraise the situation differently, or have feedback that is useful. In any case, talking to another person should always be a top priority in these situations.

Second, when it comes to some of the "negative" strategies discussed earlier, such as eating food and drinking alcohol, it is fine to use these for coping, as long as it is done in moderation. It is also probably best to do these things with other people. So, eating an entire cake or having some beers with your friends is fine, as long as it is not the only coping tool you have, and as long as it doesn't persist over a long period of time. Weight gain and hangovers are more likely to decrease your mood than give you a healthy boost. Deciding whether to use this strategy also involves knowing your own weaknesses and vulnerabilities. If you are someone with a history of substance abuse or overeating, then you might want to consider avoiding these activities in favour of others.

Third, as mentioned earlier in the book, people sometimes choose to isolate themselves following rejection, particularly if there is sadness or depression. I consider such behaviour to reflect an evolutionary purpose – an attempt to escape from whatever is causing pain (i.e., people). Similar to point #2, spending time alone is fine, as long as it is done in moderation and in conjunction with other coping strategies. Spending a day or two lying in bed, or watching TV in your pajamas is fine and sometimes comforting in and of itself. Just make sure to balance alone time with time spent with others.

Fourth, distraction is a psychological strategy that has good empirical support – again, in moderation. Whenever you are feeling sad, anxious or hurt, engaging in a pleasurable or enjoyable activity can be helpful. These activities help take your mind off the problem, which can have the added bonus of decreasing the strength of the pain and negative emotions. Distraction can be particularly useful for dealing with anger. It is important that I be very clear about what I mean by distraction. *I do not mean suppressing thoughts about the problem.* Suppressing thoughts is usually a counterproductive approach. When I use the term distraction, I mean doing something active. The best activities are those that are enjoyable and those that bring a sense of mastery and control (i.e., doing something you are good at).

Fifth, deep breathing is an exercise that can help to calm the body and the mind. There is a science to deep breathing, in terms of how it affects the physiology of the body (ex: its effect on the ratio of oxygen and carbon dioxide in the blood), but this need not be reviewed here. It is only important to know that deep breathing can calm anxiety and bring a sense of comfort. Deep breathing is fairly simple to do, although there are a few guidelines that should be followed. My advice is to do the following:

1.   Start by taking a slow and deep breath into the body, sending the air to the diaphragm. Place one hand on your chest, and one on your abdomen. A deep, diaphragmatic breath should cause your belly to blow up like a balloon, while your chest remains stable. This is actually the opposite of how most of us breathe – so it takes practice! Focus on expanding your belly when you inhale to get the most benefit. The deep in-breath should be slow.

2. Once the in-breathe has stopped, hold the breathe for 2 seconds, then

3. Exhale slowly. It is very important to slow down the out-breath – even slower than the inhale. Therefore, if your in-breath took 5 seconds, make the out-breath 6 seconds. Try to make sure you empty your lungs completely – this takes practice, too!

4. Once you've exhaled completely, hold for two seconds and repeat.

5. Knowing how long to do deep breathing is idiosyncratic in nature, and requires practice to know what your body needs. For some people, they only need 3-4 deep breaths to reduce their anger or anxiety from a 7/10 to a 3/10. For other people, they need at least 5 minutes of deep breathing to feel calm and relaxed.

6. *There is no correct way to breathe.* The guidelines presented here are just that – guidelines – not rules to be followed rigidly. As long as you slow your breathing, and focus on expanding your belly, this exercise should have positive physiological effects.

Finally, in addition to deep breathing, there are other natural ways to calm the physiology and muscle tension that comes with negative emotions and stress. Taking a bath, exercising, and going for a massage are just a few things that can help make you feel better.

Just to reiterate (because I think it is very important), *the more coping strategies you use, the better.* If following a serious relationship break-up, a falling out with a friend, or a heated argument, you can use most of these strategies, it will help make living with the pain more bearable and manageable. You must remember that the goal is not to control the pain, stress, or negative emotions. The goal is not to bring a pain rating from 9/10 to 0/10. The goal is to decrease the pain and negative feelings to a more manageable level. However, there will be some residual pain, some sadness and some negative thoughts that remain. It's OK. They will go away with time, and with the problem-solving strategies discussed earlier. You have to learn to live with some amount of unpleasantness and discomfort. Remember, it will make you a stronger person in the end.

The other recommended strategy for dealing with the pain and negative feelings is to use some of the cognitive strategies discussed earlier in the chapter. Even if you were rejected for some negative quality or mistake you made, it is important to keep things in perspective and make healthy interpretations about what this means about you as a person. Having flaws and making mistakes is very normal. And being rejected is normal as well. Did you think you would go through life and have the people that are closest to you always be pleased with everything you do? Rejection happens. It's how you handle the rejection that counts.

Rejection Involving Those We Are Not Close With

The three goals that were recommended for coping with rejection in the previous section are the same goals as those in the current section. As such, a number of the strategies that were described in the previous section are applicable here, and therefore won't be reviewed again. For example, the strategies that can be used for managing the immediate pain and negative feelings of rejection are basically the same regardless of who caused the rejection. However, when you do not know somebody well, the process of trying to understand the rejection, and efforts to problem-solve, are going to operate in a different manner.

One of the more popular and common forms of rejection is that of romantic rejection, and in particular, asking someone for a date and being turned down. I will use this simple example to highlight strategies for dealing with this kind of "stranger" rejection, although these strategies do generalize to other types of rejection as well (ex: unsuccessfully trying to make friends with someone).

When we are rejected by someone close to us, and in such a way that makes us concerned about the relationship or our behaviour, we can take the time to talk about our concerns with this person. Hopefully, if there is a problem in such a situation, we can then decide how to fix the problem. Thus, problem-solving can be a collaborative effort. When it comes to rejection from a stranger, we are mostly left to own devices in terms of dealing with the situation. This is because it is usually not appropriate to have such important and intimate conversations with strangers – and it is also fairly useless. It is useless because (1) there is no relationship worth protecting in this situation, and (2) relative strangers are often not a great source of objective information, unlike friends and family. In fact, it may even be counterproductive.

For example, if you are ever turned down for a date, there is no need to have a discussion for the sake of protecting the relationship – because there is no relationship. The only concern in this situation is why you were rejected. The reason for the rejection may or may not be important information. If the reason for the rejection stems from a longstanding personal problem, then it would be important to have access to this information. For example, if there was some problem with the way you communicated (ex: talking in an arrogant manner) or behaved (ex: making inappropriate jokes or comments), then you could make a change.

However, if you were rejected for reasons that were specific to that person, then it doesn't really matter why you were rejected. If someone doesn't find you attractive, or funny, or nice, etc., but other people see these qualities in you, then everything is fine. In this circumstance, there is no serious problem because you have qualities that are likeable and attractive to others, just not to this *particular person*. Although it may hurt to have this person reject you, you must keep things in a realistic perspective – you can't be liked by everyone. Let me repeat that because it is very important – *you cannot and will not be liked by everyone*. Now, many people know this statement is true, yet act as though it were not – they believe on some level that they can and will be liked and accepted by everyone. Let me explain why it is impossible to be liked by everyone.

It is impossible to be liked by everyone for a number of reasons, although the most important reason is this:

The specific qualities that make you likeable to some people are the exact same qualities that make you unlikeable to other people.

For example, if Norah is at a party and acting very sociably (i.e., walking around and talking to everyone), some people will think "I really like Norah – she is so friendly and confident." Yet, other people will think "I don't like Norah – she is such an attention seeker." Or, if Norah was more shy and reserved, some people would say "I really like Norah, she seems so sweet." And other people would say "I don't like Norah, she acts like she's better than everyone else." Norah can't win everyone over, and neither will you.

One of my favourite supervisors used to use the following story to make this point. He recalled that following Mother Teresa's death, there were numerous stories about her many kind deeds and charity, as there should have been. However, there were also stories that questioned her true intentions. Mother Teresa became an internationally renowned and revered figure, and so some people criticized her for doing great deeds in order to be admired by others. I mean, if Mother Teresa can't be liked by everyone, who can?

In the end, you basically have two choices: (1) you can simply be yourself, knowing that not everyone will like you, or (2) you can try to constantly change who you are to please everyone around you. I highly recommend you avoid the latter option. Constantly trying to change your behaviour to suit the preferences of other people will, over time, only leave you feeling disconnected and uncertain about who you are as a person. This is essentially what happens when people try to constantly overcompensate. It is not healthy to continually present yourself in a disingenuous fashion. You can lose a sense of self-understanding, and you also never learn to live

122

with and accept your flaws. Furthermore, people may never get an opportunity to really know who you are as a person. Finally, trying to be liked by everyone is doomed to fail. There will always be some people who just don't like you, and it will often have more to do with their specific psychological profile, as opposed to some flaw in you.

For some people, they might not care whether everyone likes them, but they are concerned about having certain traits validated. Some people have a strong need to be considered attractive. Others have a strong need to be considered smart, whereas others need to be funny. It is fine to want other people to like these qualities, as long as your expectations are reasonable. Similar to problems with needing to be liked by everyone, expecting everyone to consider you attractive, smart, and/or funny is simply unrealistic. Brad Pitt and Angelina Jolie are known for being very beautiful, yet I've met some people who do not find them especially attractive. It is usually due to some idiosyncratic preference on the part of the evaluator (ex: they don't find Ms. Jolie attractive because they find that her lips are just too big). Not everyone finds Jerry Seinfeld funny, but this doesn't mean that he isn't.

When it comes to self-evaluation, we often need other people to help us learn who we are as people. For example, I can only know that I am funny if other people laugh at my jokes. Feedback from others plays a crucial role in self-concept development. If people laugh at my jokes, it will be reasonable for me to assume that I can be funny. If some people flirt with me, I can assume that I am somewhat attractive. This form of self-learning is normal and happens to everyone. Unfortunately, as with many normal psychological processes, problems can and do inevitably arise. It is important to remember that just because a few people don't laugh at your jokes or make a pass at you does not mean that you aren't funny or attractive – it just highlights my earlier point, that you can't please everyone.

A common problem that arises with self-learning and self-evaluation occurs when a single event is overgeneralized. When wanting to know whether you have a particular quality or trait, you have to consider *all* of the evidence. If people have dated you in the past, flirted with you, and given you compliments, then it is inaccurate to think "I'm unattractive" after being turned down for a date. First, thinking of traits like attractiveness, intelligence and humour in black-or-white terms (ex: You're either pretty or you're ugly) is biased thinking that misrepresents reality. Second, you are ignoring important evidence to the contrary.

Another mistake that people sometimes make is to set the standard too high. For example (as discussed in Chapter 3), if you rate your attractiveness as being a 7/10, yet feel depressed because it is not a 9/10, then you have a problem with your standards. Therefore, when it comes to assessing how likeable you are, such assessments can reach inaccurate conclusions when the standard is unreasonable. To be considered funny or smart, you do not need to be in the top 5% of the population.

Many of the clients I see in therapy have unrealistic standards for themselves. For example, you can rate most traits on a scale from 0 (complete absence of trait) to 10 (no one is higher than you on this trait). Using this scale, 5/10 would be the average, meaning the majority of people in the world will score somewhere between 3 and 7 for most traits. It should be uncommon for people to fall in the 8-10 range, although this will occur for a few traits (i.e., a strength). It would also be uncommon for people to fall in the 0-3 range. Despite this fact, I would estimate that most people in North America would feel hurt or criticized if someone rated them as being less than a 6 on an *important* trait. Most people would probably be insulted if you rated their attractiveness or intelligence (generally speaking, two highly valued traits) as being a 5/10. In this case, you are technically saying to this person – "I think your attractiveness or intelligence is about the same as most other people". And technically speaking, this should not be a bad thing. Unfortunately, North America is a society where it is more important to stand out than to fit in, and so unreasonable standards cause significant problems for many people.

This discussion of self-evaluation is a bit off track from the main topic (i.e., handling rejection from relative strangers), but I felt it important to discuss here because I've found that many people struggle with self-concepts that shift according to changes in their social experiences. They feel confident one day, and then feel sad and hurt because of an isolated incident involving a relative stranger(s). Taking the time to accurately understand the meaning of a rejection can help prevent such dramatic changes in self-perception. And having a realistic standard by which to evaluate yourself will make determining how likeable you are more healthy and accurate.

Getting back to the goals discussed earlier, the only information that is particularly important following a rejection by a stranger is whether it represents a fundamental flaw of some sort. Was this rejection a symptom of a bigger problem? Unfortunately, answering this question can be a difficult task. As mentioned, unlike people you know, it is often inappropriate just to ask strangers to identify the problem. However, this does not mean you are completely left in the dark. If you truly are concerned that there might be a serious problem with your behaviour, then there are a few sources of information available to you

First, you can try to identify trends and patterns in your life. Do most people reject you? Are most efforts to make friends met with rejection? Have several people commented on a particular flaw? The answers to these questions can help you determine if there is a problem present. Your second option, if you earnestly want to know if there are serious problems, is to ask people who know you well. You may not always get an honest answer because friends and family members may want to avoid hurting your feelings. But if you can convince them that their input is important, and assure them that this is not simply a request for reassurance, then it might encourage greater honesty. Another potential source of objective information is a mental health professional.

Once you have a solid understanding of the problem, then you must make efforts to fix it. Fixing the problem could entail something relatively simple – like stopping a particular behaviour (ex: if you tend to drink too much at social events, then assuming there's no problem with addiction, you can better manage your drinking behaviour). However, some problems are more complex, and may require help from a professional. For example, if you have more serious problems related to social skills or difficulty controlling anger, then the services of a psychologist might be required.

Remember, *the goal of identifying personal flaws is not to correct everything and become more perfect.* You should only be looking to fix those things that cause serious problems in relationships, or problems that make forming relationships more difficult. I highly recommend that you take time to assess whether there is a *legitimate problem* before making changes. Remember, everybody has flaws, and you are no exception. You won't get rid of all of them, nor would you want to! A perfect person is not a relatable person. And there is nothing terribly wrong with being below average on a particular trait. Likeability is determined by numerous traits[32]. Otherwise, many people would be unlikeable, as we all have traits that are relative weaknesses.

In sum, the strategies reviewed in this section are practical in nature. As a psychologist, I believe that pain of any kind (physical or emotional) often has a purpose. Pain is usually a signal to focus our attention on a particular problem. Sometimes intervention will be required in response to pain, and sometimes it will not. If we have a mild headache or have been turned down for a date, then simply tolerating the pain and moving on is sometimes all that is required. But if there is a broken bone or an underlying problem with a relationship or the person, then a different type of intervention is needed.

Problems with Planning for the Future

As discussed in Chapter 5, people can develop beliefs, behaviour patterns and/or personality styles that reflect attempts to prevent and avoid rejection. Overcompensation, avoidance and passive acceptance represent various ways of trying to control and avoid rejection. With each of these response styles, there is at least one underlying negative belief present – something that significantly casts doubt on one's likeability (the ultimate core belief). Inevitably, successful, long-term treatment for these response styles is dependent on the ability to change the underlying core belief(s). For example, if someone believes that they are inherently inadequate or incompetent or unintelligent, etc., then they are more likely to undervalue their overall likeability.

When someone believes there are problems with being liked and accepted by other people, they will act in ways to protect themselves. Thus, to change these protective response styles, you have to change the underlying beliefs – both specific negative beliefs (ex: "I am incompetent") and the general likeability belief.

The thoughts, perceptions and behaviours of people with one or more of the protective response styles prevent changes in beliefs from occurring. Indeed, the primary focus of this section will be highlighting the self-sustaining nature of these response styles, and reviewing how to make permanent changes. However, prior to moving forward, it is important that I make something clear for the readers. If there is a serious, longstanding problem with one or more of these response styles, it is probably true that working with a mental health professional, such as a psychologist, is going to be necessary to make long-lasting change. When a serious psychological issue is present, it often takes more than a book to fix the problem.

In order to describe how coping response styles are self-sustaining, I am going to use an example involving overcompensation. In fact, it will be easier to stick with the example I used in Chapter 5 – Ted. As a quick reminder, Ted developed negative core beliefs about himself during a very awkward phase of development in high school. He subsequently overcompensated for these negative beliefs focusing heavily on career success and physical appearance.

First, I would like to reiterate that Ted's response to the pain of rejection and unlikeability in high school is understandable. It was a very difficult period of time and he felt that developing strengths would help him to cope. However, ideally speaking, Ted should have eventually recognized that his core beliefs were both exaggerated and context-dependent. Being picked on and having your flaws highlighted by others is always difficult, and especially so during high school. When in such a difficult situation, one cannot help but wonder why these problems are occurring and how to fix them. It is the 'why' part that is often difficult to completely understand with an objective frame of mind. When you consider yourself to be unattractive while spending most of your time in a social environment where physical attractiveness is valued, it is difficult not to think of yourself as unlikeable to some degree. Similarly, if you believe that you are unintelligent and live in an environment where this trait is highly valued, it can certainly affect self-estimations of likeability. The pattern here is that our immediate social environments can significantly influence how likeable we believe we are.

The unfortunate aspect of being in a social environment where you lack the qualities valued by the group is that you end up feeling unlikeable and rejected. And there may be an element of truth to this feeling. If in high school you possessed traits that made you unlikeable to many other students, you would technically be unlikeable and rejected. This is why many people would have empathy for someone like Ted – they are essentially forced to endure being in an environment that has the potential for much painful rejection and feelings of low self-worth. However, just because you are not well-liked in one particular environment does not mean you are unlikeable as a person. This is a lesson that many high school students learn when they move onto college and eventually the work force. The social environments of college and the workplace are usually quite different from that of high school. Suddenly, the narrow range of qualities that were valued in high school are broadened considerably, and people are liked for more than being attractive or athletic. Also, in the case of Ted, his problems with physical appearance were time-specific – just an awkward developmental phase. However, rather than perceive his social difficulties as being context-specific, he continues to see himself as awkward and unlikeable. Why?

Ted's efforts to 'fix' his problems were classified as overcompensation because they were a persistent attempt to improve his likeability by altering certain traits. He made these changes with the intention of improving his likeability. There are two problems with this approach – one more severe than the other. First, he never really had to make such major changes. Once high school ended and he changed his social environment, he probably would have noticed improvement in how he was treated without making any changes to himself. If he had also made some other minor changes to improve his physical appearance this probably would have been sufficient, healthy and acceptable. Unfortunately, he believed that drastic changes were needed, and he spent much of his life striving to be the perfect male.

The second problem with Ted's attempt to change his likeability is how extended the effort has been. As I previously stated, it is understandable that Ted would want to make some changes in order to cope with *that period of time in his life*. This would not be so bad if he eventually let go of these overcompensating behaviours. Unfortunately, he has held onto them for an extended period of time. This really highlights how self-sustaining such changes can be. If Ted could put into words the process of change that has occurred for him, it would look something like this:

There was clearly something wrong with me. There were aspects of who I am that made me unacceptable to other people. Because I am unlikeable the way I am, I had to make some big changes. These big changes that I made caused more people to like me and I no longer have to deal with the pain of rejection that was so awful in high school. People like me now because I am successful, attractive and confident. I have to keep these qualities in order to keep people from seeing the unlikeable things about me. If people saw my flaws, it would be like high school all over again. If people don't like me the way I am, I simply have to be someone they will like.

The positive association between the changes Ted has made and the positive attention/ lack of rejection maintains his behaviour. He is under the impression that people like him for relatively superficial qualities. He predicts that these positive qualities must be maintained in order to be likeable, and that flaws and imperfections only increase the potential for rejection. Many of the clients that I have seen who overcompensate in this way have told me that they feel like they're wearing a mask. It's as if everyone is looking at a character they created for the world to see – but this character is fake. The real person underneath the mask has flaws and imperfections and would be rejected if the mask were taken off. This leaves people like Ted in a difficult position. If you wear the mask, you receive positive evaluations from others and avoid rejection. Unfortunately, by keeping the mask on you feel like a fraud – alienated from yourself and others. Intimate relationships are less likely to succeed because true connections require that the mask be removed. Conversely, if you remove the mask and show others your flaws, there is risk of being rejected, and those painful thoughts and feelings from the past will come flooding back.

This dilemma takes us back to an earlier part of this book, when I explained how people are often motivated to make the safe choice. In this case, the safe choice is to keep wearing the mask. If Ted were to spend the rest of his life trying to be someone that many people would like (from a distance), he would undoubtedly experience less rejection. It's the safest path to take. This explains why core beliefs and personality styles like overcompensation are self-sustaining – they serve a very useful function.

In order to change personality styles, there must be change in the core beliefs. When a person no longer believes they are inherently unlikeable, there is no further need for overcompensation. When you believe that you are, for the most part, a likeable person, there is no need for a mask or any other form of protection. When you no longer believe that people are highly prone to hurt you (through forms of rejection), there will no longer be a need to hide or protect yourself from them. So, how do you change beliefs?

A helpful first step toward change in this situation is to recognize and understand as best you can your own psychological profile. Examining the past and understanding how certain beliefs formed, why various behaviours developed, and how these factors operate in a self-sustaining manner is important. It allows you to see things in their appropriate context. If you are someone who developed negative beliefs because of hurtful experiences earlier in life, then it will be important to understand that problems from a particular period of time do not generalize across life. For example, if you were heavily criticized by a teacher, it does not mean you are unintelligent. If you were rejected in high school, it does not mean you are unlikeable. There are factors specific to that period in your life that are no longer relevant.

However, do not get too hung up on the past. Insight into the origins of psychological problems is not sufficient for change, which is why treatments that focus only on the past are rarely helpful in the long-run. Good change often requires action. As such, I would recommend that cognitive and behavioural strategies be used to help make lasting changes.

As discussed earlier in this chapter, CBT is a form of therapy that places a lot of value and importance on evidence. If you want to evaluate whether you are likeable, or whether some other quality is present, you can evaluate it by examining the facts. This task can be accomplished by simply listing the evidence for and against a particular idea. For example, if you want to know if you are likeable, you can evaluate the evidence for and against this idea. The goal is not to walk away from such an exercise thinking "I am 100% likeable." In fact, following such an exercise, it is often likely that people start to realize that they are neither completely likeable nor unlikeable. Rather, after examining evidence for and against the possibility of being a likeable person, people usually come to learn something like this: "Although not everyone likes me, there are many people who do." At the end of the day, being liked by some people is all you really need.

One of the difficulties with examining the evidence is that some people find such an evaluation nearly impossible. People who overcompensate don't know if the "real" them is likeable because they've been hiding this person for a significant period of time. People who are avoiders don't know because they haven't really given themselves an honest chance of being liked and connecting with other people. Therefore, behavioural change will be necessary.

The major response styles discussed in Chapter 5 were basically descriptions of defence mechanisms – strategies used by people to prevent something psychologically harmful from happening. Each of the response styles are designed to prevent and avoid the pain of rejection. When defences are up, there can be no change in beliefs. When you start to remove the defences slowly over time, you get a chance to test your underlying beliefs, fears and associated predictions. For example, the following are predictions that someone with a core belief of unlikeability might hold (the defence mechanism is in brackets):

- "If I talk to someone at a party, they will become bored and try to leave and talk to someone else." (At social events, keep quiet).

- "When I start dating someone, they will think I'm awkward and eventually leave me." (Avoid close relationships)

- "If I discuss a personal problem with someone, they will think less of me." (Help others, but don't allow anyone to help you)

- "If someone sees my flaws, it will harm the relationship." (Hide all flaws and imperfection)

- "No one will ever want to be a really close friend – only an acquaintance." (Avoid taking steps to develop meaningful friendships)

- "I'm not going to ask my co-worker to grab a coffee after work because they will just find an excuse to reject me." (Don't take a risk and wait/hope someone asks me to go for a coffee)

These are just a few examples from a vast array of negative predictions and expectations that can occur on a daily basis for someone with negative beliefs about their likeability. As long as the unlikeability belief exists, the negative predictions will remain. As long as the negative predictions exist, the person will feel compelled to protect themselves with defence mechanisms. So, to change the underlying belief, we have to start dropping the defences. This typically involves identifying a negative prediction and testing it out. If you predict that people will reject you if they see your flaws, then you must think of various ways that you can show your flaws and be imperfect. It is usually best to do something like this in a gradual manner, starting with something easy (i.e., showing a flaw that you are not overly concerned about) and moving toward difficult tasks (ex: being in a close relationship and discussing things that are highly personal and important). I believe that such behavioural experiments are best accomplished with the help of an objective third party – like a mental health professional.

One of the potential problems with behavioural experiments and dropping defences is having the courage to try them. This is particularly true for someone who has held certain defences for a long period of time. Typically, this group of people strongly overestimates how likely rejection is to occur, how painful the rejection will feel, and how incapable they will be in terms of coping. Such predictions are part of the unlikeability belief system and they must be addressed and corrected. Unless there is an actual, serious problem with likeability and rejection, people with unlikeability beliefs almost always overestimate problems in this area. Testing these predictions is the most productive method for change. By dropping defences gradually and testing predictions, the person in question can learn that rejection occurs and it hurts – but the picture is not nearly as bad as they think. Similarly, unless there is a serious problem with coping, this group of people typically handle the pain of rejection better than they think.

So, what happens if someone is actually unlikeable, often gets rejected and/ or has serious problems with coping? When this is the case, working with a professional is almost mandatory for real change to occur. Some of the more common reasons for unlikeability are:

- **Underdeveloped social skills** (ex: constantly interrupting and making inappropriate comments during conversations)
- **Aggressive interpersonal style** (ex: being overly critical and demanding of everyone)

134

- **Overly dependent interpersonal style** (ex: constant need to be with another person/ other people, leaving little independence for loved ones)
- **Serious problems with insecurity** (ex: constant reassurance-seeking)
- **Selfish/Egotistic** (ex: constantly putting own needs ahead of those of other people)

These are some of the more common reasons for interpersonal problems, rejection and unlikeability. If it can be determined that such problems exist, and that they are interfering with a person's quality of life, then I highly recommend some type of professional help. Similarly, if someone has a problem with coping with rejection, then professional services are recommended as well. As outlined in Chapter 4, unhealthy responses to rejection can often make matters worse.

Concluding Message: Keeping Things in Perspective

My daily interactions with clients who struggle with both rejection and concerns about likeability played an important role in motivating me to write this book. Knowing the important role that interpersonal relationships play in mental health and quality of life, it can be very difficult watching someone experience such difficult problems. One of the more discouraging and difficult aspects of my job is watching people who have many positive qualities and features make so many mistakes when it comes to self-evaluation. It is difficult hearing a bright, kind, and caring client describe him/herself as "stupid" and "worthless."

I believe that part of the problem is cultural. In North America today, there is a strong emphasis on superficial qualities, which people can easily misinterpret to mean that such traits are the most important. Magazines, television shows, and movies have the potential to significantly distort people's self-beliefs by artificially changing the value of certain qualities, such as attractiveness and social status. For the most part, the emphasis on superficiality comes from advertisers whose main goal is to sell something to an audience. When you associate things that are considered positive (ex: beautiful people; money; popularity) with things that are relatively neutral (ex: beer; movie or TV show promotion; magazines), you can make the neutral object more positive. This is called *evaluative conditioning* and it is a staple of advertising. Unfortunately, people don't always consciously consider the purpose of the advertising - they only see the end product. Over time, the importance of these positive, yet superficial qualities becomes inflated, and people mistakenly overvalue them in terms of being liked by others.

Many of the clients I work with end up selecting a very narrow list of qualities as important and necessary for likeability. In their opinion, these qualities are either absent or not "strong" enough (ex; "I know I'm slightly above average in terms of attractiveness, but I want to be beautiful"). Indeed, in North America, things have gotten to the point where "average" is a bad thing – a criticism at times. Being like other people is viewed negatively, and people strive to stand out in some way – just like the people on TV and in magazines.

When it comes to being liked, you must rid yourself of any beliefs that require you to possess one or two superficial strengths to be liked. There are a host of qualities that make people likeable and attractive to other people. Indeed, research shows that things like physical attractiveness, money, and social status are never at the top of the list of qualities that people seek out in others[33]. The most desired qualities tend to be warmth and kindness, sense of humour, and being open and expressive. Being nice is boring relative to being sexy or brilliant, but it is a necessary quality for being likeable (while being sexy is not). You don't even have to be the nicest person in the world – which brings me to my final point.

Being average is something that many people want to avoid. They don't equate average with likeable. Personally and professionally, I believe that being comfortable with average is a very healthy way to live. This does not mean you cannot have strengths. Perhaps you are above-average in a skill (ex: drawing), intelligence, sense of humour, etc. – this is great! Such strengths can bring confidence and other rewards. However, strengths are not necessary to be likeable, not necessary for having healthy relationships, and not necessary for being happy. I sometimes think that North Americans confuse being "liked" with being "admired." If your goal is to be admired or adored, then you will need to have an incredible talent, ability or quality/trait. But being admired has nothing to do with happiness, relationships or quality of life. Conversely, being liked by other people *is associated* with happiness and quality of life – through our involvement in healthy relationships.

At the end of the day, being liked is often easier than people think, and by extension, so is finding happiness through others.

References

[1] Leary, M.R. Sociometer theory and the pursuit of relational value: Getting to the root of self-esteem. *European Review of Social Psychology, 16*, 75-111.

[2] See Ohman. A. (2005). The role of the amygdala in human fear: Automatic detection of threat. *Psychoneuroendocrinology 30*, 953–958.

[3] Melzack, R., & Wall, P. D. (1996). *The challenge of pain* (3rd ed.).London: Penguin.

[4] Baumeister, R.F. & Leary, M.R. (1995). The need to belong: Desire for interpersonal attachment as a fundamental human motivation. *Psychological Bulleting, 117*, 497-529

[5] MacDonald, G. & Leary, M.R. (2005). Why does social exclusion hurt? The relationship between social and physical pain. *Psychological Bulletin, 131*, 202-223.

[6] Leary, M.R., Twenge, J.M., & Quinlivan, E. (2006). Interpersonal rejection as a determinant of anger and aggression. *Personality and Social Psychology Review, 10*, 111-132.

[7] Palermo, R. & Rhodes, G. (2007). Are you always on my mind? A review of how face perception and attention interact. *Neuropsychologia 45*, 75-92.

[8] Ford, M.B. & Collins, N.L. (2010). Self-esteem moderates neuroendocrine and psychological responses to interpersonal rejection. *Journal of Personality and Social Psychology, 98*, 405-419.

[9] Rapee, R.M. & Heimberg, R.G. (1997). A cognitive-behavioral model of anxiety in social phobia. *Behaviour, Research and Therapy, 35*, 741-756.

[10] MacDonald & Leary (2005).

[11] MacDonald & Leary (2005).

[12] Keiichi, O. et al. (2009). Decreased ventral anterior cingulate cortex activity is associated with reduced social pain during emotional support. *Social Neuroscience, 4*, 443-454.

[13] Leary et al. (2006).

[14] Allen, N.B. & Badcock, P.B.T. (2003). The social risk hypothesis of depressed mood: Evolutionary, psychosocial, and neurobiological perspectives. *Psychological Bulletin, 129*, 887-913.

[15] Brown, J.L., Sheffield, D., Leary, M.R., & Robinson, M.E. (2003). Social support and experimental pain. *Psychosomatic Medicine, 65,* 276-283.

[16] Brinker, J.K. & Dozois, D.J.A. (2009). Ruminative thought style and depressed mood. *Journal of Clinical Psychology, 65,* 1-19.

[17] Beck, A.T. (1976). *Cognitive therapy and the emotional disorders.* New York: International University Press.

[18] Gawronski, B., & Bodenhausen, G.V. (2006). Associative and propositional processes in evaluation: An integrative review of implicit and explicit attitude change. *Psychological Bulletin, 132,* 692-731.

[19] Leary et al. (2006).

[20] Leary et al. (2006).

[21] Allen & Badcock (2003).

[22] Nolen-Hoeksema, S. (2000). The role of rumination in depressive disorder and mixed anxiety/ depressive symptoms. *Journal of Abnormal Psychology, 109,* 504-511.

[23] Morgan, J. (2010). Autobiographical memory biases in social anxiety. *Clinical Psychology Review, 30,* 288-297.

[24] Young, J.E., Klosko, J.S., & Weishaar, M.E. (2003). *Schema Therapy: A practitioner's guide.* New York: Guilford.

[25] Young et al. (2003).

[26] Young et al. (2003).

[27] Westen, D. (1998). The scientific legacy of Sigmund Freud: Toward a psychodynamically informed psychological science. *Psychological Bulletin, 124,* 333-371.

[28] Dijksterhuis, Ap (2004). I like myself but I don't know why: Enhancing implicit self-esteem by subliminal evaluative conditioning. *Journal of Personality and Social Psychology, 86,* 345-355.

[29] Butler, A.C., Chapman, J.E., Forman, E.M., & Beck, A.T. (2006). The empirical status of cognitive-behavioral therapy: A review of meta-analyses. *Clinical Psychology Review, 26,* 17-31.

[30] Covin, R., Dozois, D.J.A., Seeds, P.M., & Ogniewicz, A. (in press). Measuring cognitive errors: Initial development of the Cognitive Distortions Scale (CDS). *International Journal of Cognitive Therapy.*

[31] Loehr, J. & Schwartz, T. (2004). *The power of full engagement: Managing energy, not time, is the key to high performance and personal renewal.* New York: Free Press.

[32] Sprecher & Regan. (2002). Liking some things (in some people) more than others: Partner preferences in romantic relationships and friendships. *Journal of Social and Personal Relationships, 19*, 463-481.

[33] Sprecher & Regan. (2002).

19284223R00084

Made in the USA
San Bernardino, CA
19 February 2015